The Time is Now
For a Better Life and a Better World

The Time is Now
For a Better Life and a Better World

By
HUA-CHING NI
Teacher of the One Great Path of Subtle Truth

The Shrine of the Eternal Breath of Tao
College of Tao & Traditional Chinese Healing
SANTA MONICA

*Thanks and appreciation to Suta Cahill,
Janet DeCourtney, Frank Gibson and the mentors
of the Center for Taoist Arts for typing,
proofreading, editing and typesetting this book.*

Shrine of the Eternal Breath of Tao
College of Tao and Traditional Chinese Healing,
1314 Second Street #208, Santa Monica, CA 90401

Library of Congress Catalog Card No. 92-50854
ISBN 0-937064-63-7

*Dedicated to those who are aware
that it is time to return
to the One Great Path of Subtle Truth
and work on practical improvement
for a better life and better world.*

To female readers,

According to natural spiritual teaching, male and female are equally important in the natural sphere. This is seen in the diagram of T'ai Chi. Thus, discrimination is not practiced in our tradition. All my work is dedicated to both genders of human people.

Wherever possible, constructions using masculine pronouns to represent both sexes are avoided; where they occur, we ask your tolerance and spiritual understanding. We hope that you will take the essence of my teaching and overlook the superficiality of language. Gender discrimination is inherent in English; ancient Chinese pronouns do not have differences of gender. I wish that all of you achieve above the level of language or gender.

Thank you, H. C. Ni

Contents

Prelude

The Subtle Essence conveyed by the teaching of the Integral Way is the deep truth of all religions, yet it transcends all religions, leaving them behind as clothing worn in different seasons or places. The teaching of the Subtle Essence includes everything of religious importance, yet it goes beyond the level of religion. It directly serves your life, surpassing the boundary of all religions and extracting the essence of them all.

The Subtle Essence as conveyed by the teaching of the Integral Way is also the goal of all sciences, but it surpasses all sciences, leaving them behind as partial and temporal descriptions of this universal Integral Truth. Unlike any partial science, the Way goes beyond the level of any single scientific search.

The Subtle Essence is the master teaching. It does not rely on any authority. It is like a master key which can unlock all doors directly leading you to the inner room of the ultimate truth. It is not frozen at the emotional surface of life. It does not remain locked at the level of thought or belief with the struggling which extends to skepticism and endless searching.

The teaching of the One Great Path of the Subtle Essence presents the core of the Integral Truth and helps you reach it yourself.

The Teaching of the Integral Way

Master Ni's teaching:

T   *stands for Truth*

A   *stands for Above*

O   *stands for Oneself*

Thus, Tao stands for
TRUTH ABOVE ONESELF.

Also,

T   *stands for Truth*

A   *stands for Among*

O   *stands for Ourselves*

Thus, at the same time, Tao stands for
TRUTH AMONG OURSELVES.

Chapter 1

Nature Speaks

Preface

It is time for all of us to examine the world in order to see the future. During the past 3,000 years, humankind has applied its intelligence toward developing different religions and religious sects in order to organize a better spiritual life. However, these attempts were only responses to the emotional need of a time and a people on either a small or a big scale.

Some people have applied their intellectual strength in a totally different direction. Inventions and creations in the material sphere can help us broaden our vision to understand life, which is composed of physical form, intellectual strength and spiritual function. A good life cannot be experienced without the balance of these three. This proves the ancient teaching of the *I Ching* and the *Tao Teh Ching*, which are guides for safe development and health.

It is time for us to recognize that past religious creations have done their job of helping the growth of people in different regions and epochs. It is time for people to outgrow old social and religious customs in order to draw nearer to a happy future.

We cannot expect the world not to change. In the past, all the sages and prophets have warned us to face the reality that the physical world is not everlasting. Zoroaster taught it first, then Sakyamuni, Jesus and Mohammed. The great Chuang Tzu taught that everything is made equal by the natural process of transformation. Then there are also Lao Tzu and many other great sages.

We need to listen to the warning of the sages. We are not deaf, blind or dumb; we are sensible. We also have good intellectual strength and strong spiritual energy. Therefore, it is time for us to come together to work out our future. Spiritual integration is one important step. For spiritual support and emotional help, different religions and customs can serve you on some level, but we need to respect spiritual unity as the essence above all religious expressions.

We have faced the increasing threat of natural, social and individual crises. Should these crises not awaken us to transcend our personal interests and devote ourselves to the greater work of the larger environment and its survival? For the better survival of all people, we must recognize the omni-present way of life which was illustrated by Lao Tzu whose teaching is non-religious, impartial and non-discriminative. The Way serves all people, all times and all places. The Way is ever-existing. It is too subtle to describe. It is too gentle to refuse. From Lao Tzu's revelation, from Jesus' teaching and from the work of all other sages and prophets, we can better see the unified spiritual truth of the world. Therefore, I have engaged in the search or exploration for the spiritual unity of the entire world. The Way is unity. It can be the universal exaltation.

I have called you to awaken to universal natural truth. We may still need spiritually developed authorities like Lao Tzu, Jesus, and others who can help us go further on our own Way.

In this booklet, you will find the contribution of two great important cultures unified as the guiding light by which all humankind can restructure their lives according to natural principle and reason.

Your spiritual friend,
Hua-Ching Ni
September 11, 1992

Chapter 2

Ocean Speaks

The talks in the next three chapters were given on September 5, 1992, the first day of the Annual Retreat of Yo San University of Traditional Chinese Medicine in Santa Monica, California.

Proclamation in the Year of the Waterside Monkey

We will soon reach the end of this millennium. During this turning point, there will be wars and earthquakes around the world. Not necessarily on an exact date, but around that time certain events will occur. Some pessimistic people are expecting doomsday and think there may not even be another millennium. I want to correct this idea. The earth reshapes itself constantly. Knowing this should give you ample time to prepare yourselves.

My teaching is the inherited life spirit of all human ancestors for many millennia. It is a spirit of positive life attitudes. We all need to take care of day-to-day matters in a positive way, and a positive attitude is the internal power that enables us to turn the wheel of fortune so that we are on a better side.

With a positive life attitude and spirit, we continue our normal life activities even during disturbances such as war, earthquakes, hurricanes, comets, etc. Each of us must be spiritually prepared at all times, because physical life does not last forever, not even the life of Mother Earth or any other heavenly body. It is important to remember, however, that the life spirit of the universe cannot be extinguished; even so, it can be nurtured by you.

I

Natural disasters such as floods, volcanic eruptions or the reshaping of the earth are not something that can be completely avoided. With our intelligence, survival or rehabilitation from these disasters is easily accomplished. On the other hand, trouble that comes from mankind itself, such as war or plagues passed through sexual contact, is usually much bigger and more dangerous. Trouble such as this can be avoided or reduced by our own spiritual discipline. The task before us now is to see whether we can reduce or diminish the deepening trouble that humankind has created for itself. We can begin by not causing any further trouble in our own lives and guiding our friends to stop fueling the force of humankind's self-destructive behavior. My own contribution is to keep teaching and writing my books. I particularly appreciate all of you who have come here to help me fulfill what needs to be done at this turning point of time.

II

For less than 2,000 years, the focus of the Chinese folk religion called Taoism has been similar to that of Hinduism. Both religions involve idol worship in exchange for personal prosperity. The people give each god or statue the name of a god. Protection is expected, but not much real growth can be attained from such religious activities because the true power of peace and prosperity is a process which works within an individual, starting from the inside and moving outward.

My teaching work is not a career, it is an offering as part of my healing work. Whether I was in mainland China, Taiwan, the United States or any other country of the West, I avoided all sects or religions in order to nourish the initiative energy as my life. Nor does my teaching represent the old religions. Instead, I offer my own personal effort as a modern example for people who are facing new difficulties and challenges. Some students and helpers have promoted me as a Taoist Master. I can be recognized as a teacher of natural truth or teacher of the Integral Way. Those terms are a more truthful presentation of what I do.

Religious Taoism, or any sect of folk Taoism, is one of many religions. It is not better or worse than other religions, past or present; yet none of them can do much to improve the world. The spiritual education I am offering is at a higher level than religions. I grew up in an open society where Buddhism, Taoism and all sects of Christianity and Islam were active. Yet it seemed that all they did was create separatism and prejudice. Have they nothing better to give the world? Some believers live on the books of religions, while others sit on or stand on them to make themselves look taller. I would rather stand on natural ground. The true spiritual heritage of my teaching is from the ancient spiritually developed ones. They did not sell any stories that would warp people's natural lives. A natural life does not need to be adorned or painted. We can enjoy a high level of civilization, with good manners and refined attitudes, without using shells to replace our essence.

Do you have any questions about what I have said so far?

Q: Master Ni, what caused people to change from living a natural way of life? After all, if it was so good, why would they want to do anything else?

Master Ni: A different culture was created. There was a sudden change in the world about 2,500 years ago. Nobody respected the old moral values any more. People only looked to see who did better; they gathered power for personal enjoyment and to control other people. Slavery started at that time. People say that we do not have slavery now, but in a certain way we are still slaves to one extent or another. Sorry for that.

Q: So today we still have some trouble, just like 2,500 years ago, right? How come we do not appreciate living a totally natural way of life?

Q: I think the natural way of life existed too far in the past. Nobody knows what it is any more. We are brought up watching television and living other people's dreams and ideas. We are lost.

Q: I think we know what it is to live a natural life, but we have trouble living a completely natural way. How can we do it? Some people think that it is going to live on a mountain, but I doubt that.

Q: I think we need stronger family values.

Master Ni: That is not a bad idea. However, the problem is not only with the family, it is pervasive because of social contact. How can you maintain family values when your children are mostly influenced by the society and the other children rather than by you?

III

At the beginning of my teaching, I used the word "Tao" frequently because it was habit. However, the Integral Way is not the same as religious folk Taoism. It is time for me to clarify the Integral Way as a time-tested, ancient spiritual culture. Although each generation has a small number of individuals who appreciate and use it, the Integral Way has never been the way of the masses or of leaders. It is only followed by those whom we might call "Integral Wayfarers."

In the last several years I have become more careful about the source of people's confusion about my teaching, especially in my use of the word "Tao," which has been usurped by many religious sects. I have simply given up using the word for the most part. When I do use it, I do not use it in the traditional way. Instead, I have newly defined "Tao" in my most recent books as the "Truth Above Oneself," and at the same time as the "Truth Among Ourselves."

The Integral Way is not necessarily a continuation of ancient Chinese culture. Such a culture had already deserted China many years ago. Truthfully, such a culture was never valued among the masses in China. Nonetheless, the Integral Way can be suitably presented as a modern renaissance which can bring about a new culture in the world. Modern "Wayfarers" in this renaissance make absolutely no insistence upon a Chinese background.

My family members and I have lived in many different places around the world. Now we are citizens of the United States, but we consider ourselves to be mainly citizens of the world. Thus, we do not belong to China either, so all the work my family, myself and all of you have done and will do is an offering to people all over the world. It has nothing to do with China, but of course, we do not exclude any Chinese people who would like to learn it.

I would not like you or anyone who learns the Integral Way to think that it has been imported from China. I would like you to think that it is something that comes from us, from you and me. The Integral Way is produced from the spiritual reaction for, by and of the modern world. I would like all of you to have this understanding.

IV

The ancient Greeks recognized two types of culture: the "god of Wine" culture and the "god of Moon" culture. Some of you might be familiar with this classification.

According to the Greek view, the last 2,000 years have been dominated by the god of Wine, or Wine-god culture. You may be interested in knowing more about it.

Let us start by using as an example some of the early Christians. However, let us please be careful here. I would like to make a clear distinction between the behavior of Jesus and the behavior of some of the people who followed him. Whatever people did after Jesus was crucified was not Jesus' personal wish. Their behavior has nothing to do with Jesus' direct teaching. In this discussion, we are not talking about Jesus himself.

Here we are talking about the early Christians. Many of them were persecuted and did not yield to that persecution. Many people died for martyrdom. This falls under the category of Wine-god culture in which people act like drunken sailors and unquestioningly plunge their lives into any direction they are told to follow.

Let us also consider the rise of Mohammed in the desert. During Mohammed's lifetime, there was a riot, and after his life ended, his followers started the fire of war everywhere. Any strong leader can amass a large number of people to engage in some activity which has a wild direction, but how much does it benefit human society in the long run? Mohammed's followers are thus a second example of the influence or nature of Wine-god culture, drunkenly throwing their lives away to kismet.[1]

As a third example, we can take the fascists in Germany and the rise of communism in several places in the world. Karl Marx attacked idealism, but was basically an idealist himself. His idealism drew many people or comrades to die for his thoughts. In today's China, this kind of idealism has produced the communist system which allows some people to enjoy special privileges. Unfortunately, once people enjoy special privileges, they suppress those who do not. That is not what Marx planned, but he did not foresee that when he began his program. Thus, in China today it is not the general public who want to preserve communism; it is the party members, government officials and bureaucracy who resist giving up their special treatment and privileges. Special privileges are why communists insist upon such idealism.

The worst result of idealism in China was the so-called Cultural Revolution that began in 1962 under the leadership of the "Gang of Four." The extremes of this wave of terror all produced or supported a cultural condition formed by the god of Wine.

Now, if a spiritual direction is exalted anywhere that follows the god of Wine, the same kind of cultural movement follows. It is not hard to find people engaging in all kinds of destructive adventure, but it is hard to find people who will become calm and stay cool so that they can look at things clearly.

---

[1] Kismet is the Arab word for fate and the Islamic belief that Allah writes your life and your duty is to surrender to your fate.

Generally speaking, there are two types of life systems: independent and dependent. Both have their defects. The independent system tends to be indifferent or lack concern for how other people are doing. The dependent system tends to rigidly reject the differences of individuals and to worry that other people might become well off.

My suggestion is to have a healthy human society in which each individual is naturally independent and creative, but searches for a cooperative way to contribute to the common good. Such a society would not reject differences in talent, personality or temperament. Mutual support would bring about a rewarding life, which would avoid conflict or confrontation between people holding different views.

For example, it is not suitable to consider homosexuality immoral. It can be considered as an internal problem of a sort of subnormal or peculiar interest. In general, we might recognize that homosexuals are normal people with some difficulty. It might be helped by herbs or other natural ingredients to restore the internal balance. Homosexual behavior not only exists among people, but also among cockroaches. In a certain stage of weather or life condition, cockroaches will become sexually excited by staring at the same sex. We can find ways to help people by establishing a study or research of the insects. It would be easy to stop the promotion of homosexual activities through pornographic books and movies, but it would be harder and more serious to consider homosexuality as a special physical phenomenon and develop a treatment. Perhaps then the AIDS problem could be uprooted and a remedy be found in the process. Homosexual tendencies might be helped by becoming vegetarians. Also, such a desire might be curtailed by putting a chewable vitamin C in the mouth and letting it melt. Those things can help.

Sexually, harmonious fulfillment is beneficial to the body, mind and spirit. The problem is that few people can have that luck. Most couples have only 30% harmony; the other 70% is personal virtuous effort to maintain the harmony. Therefore, in a natural life, the harmonious fulfillment of sex is a special privilege. People who do differently extend themselves due to lack of fulfillment.

I like talented people to come together and I like to have financial resources to support research on all useful projects. Such projects are the new direction of human intellectual power. At this time, we need to see how we can fully use human resources and financial power to benefit all people. For example, we need to redirect the use of destructive weapons such as the chemical warfare used by Iraq on Iranian villages. Such intellectual strength and financial power could be directed in a positive direction rather than toward narrow-minded competition. We all need to work for the survival of the totality of humankind.

The Integral Way is *not* the culture of the god of Wine. I think the dominance of the culture of the god of Wine that has suppressed human society for the past two thousand years needs to be finished. My suggestion is to try to extend our individual personalities and extend our society to become the culture of the god of Moon which is characterized by clarity and mildness. This represents spiritual sobriety, not barren coldness. In truth, the moon is not lifeless, even though it appears that way to some people.

When I suggest that people cool down because they are too hot, I do not mean that they need to be taken like a red-hot iron from the fire and suddenly put in water and then set aside for a thousand years. Do not become that cold. Coldness and spiritual sobriety are different. It is appropriate to cool down to be ladies and gentlemen. I think, and you might agree with me, that spiritual sobriety has its value in personal life as well as in cultural and spiritual leadership.

Many of you here are becoming more interested in helping promote the attainment of spiritual sobriety in each individual's life. If we are too cold, however, then how can we do our job? The trouble is that once a spiritual teacher teaches anything, something like coolness for example, somebody will interpret it too rigidly. I have explained to you that we like the clearness and brightness of the moon on a dark winter's night, but we also need some warmth.

The warmth in your life needs to be attuned to approximate the amount of warmth of the sun in late spring or early summer, but it should not be as strong as the heat from the summer sun, because that is too strong. Summer sun culture has been dominating the world for over 2,000 years. It should be over and finished soon.

Life returns, is nurtured and grows best during the springtime, around the end of May and beginning of June. During that time, the weather is the most productive and supportive for all lives. I need every one of you here to please remember what I say: do not be a summer sun. I do not want you to become overheated. My teaching is not meant to heat people up too much. I also would not have you become too cold like a rock from the moon, I would like you to be as warm as the May sun and as cool as the early morning air.

V

I suggest that all my students who help me develop the spiritual health of the world also work in general society to support their physical and material needs. I do not want you to give up the mainstream of life. My learning or achievement is focused upon serving people who live in the mainstream. Surely, once my students provide for their material needs from their own achievement, they will not want to overexpand this aspect of life, but would rather concentrate upon spiritual service and cultivation.

This means that students support themselves with regular work in the general world, then do spiritual work to improve the world. I am proud of the mentors who can do so, because that expresses a different virtue than the ancient type of spiritual teachers and leaders who promote spiritually intended activity for their own support. I expect mentors to do a perfect job with perfect concentration on their significant spiritual work, and I believe their teaching needs to be paid for by those who attend the classes.

Some of my Western friends who are interested in my teaching were impressed by the early stage of translation of the work of Chuang Tzu and the *Poems of Cold Mountain*. The spirit of the *Poems of Cold Mountain* has been greatly appreciated by Japanese Zahn (Zen) students. It was Zen teachers who made Cold Mountain known to Western friends. I myself also enjoyed the poems written by Cold Mountain.

In real life, however, people of the Zahn (Zen) tradition have mostly lived together as an agricultural community in China where they developed land for farming. Few Zahn temples depend on donations from society. This means they live from their own strength of life. Master Bai Tsan (Hundred Fathoms) made an especially great example by insisting upon doing labor and productive work in the field until his very old age. Many times his students and followers hid the hoe from him out of love and did not let him work. However, he did not accept that, so he started to fast. Each of his students bowed to him and requested that he eat, but he said, "If I'm not going to work that day, I'm not going to eat that day." His life illustrated that eating is the good result which comes from accomplishing your productive labor work. Eating is not meant to be a lazy pastime. His model is most respectful. This is how Zahn Buddhism came to be established and respected by people. They did not use the golden statue of Buddha to take advantage of people's lack of knowledge; they used their golden colored statues of Buddha to teach people the deep truth of a responsible, earnest life. The Zahn people, among other spiritual practitioners, truly continued the traditional spiritual virtue of the ancient spiritually developed ones which is different from the mendicant tradition of Hinduism.

At Tien Tai mountain, there was a Zahn temple in which people worked during the daytime and meditated in the evening and at night. If it was a busy day in the field, then only the basic daily ceremonies were done.

I somewhat agree that Cold Mountain and his friends, Shih Teh and Fung Kang, should have earned a laurel crown for their poems, but in their lifetime, they did not do anything but eat the leftovers from the farmer monks.

Everybody worked hard to support the community, except those one, two or three people who were talented at making poems, but did nothing for their lives. They ate only the leftovers and were not going to be bothered with life; what they did is not called living in the mainstream of life.

When I came to the United States, people expected me to present Cold Mountain. They also thought of Chuang Tzu as an ancient hippie. Actually, I am a kind of hippie who needs to earn his own bread and who would be unhappy to take somebody else's bread for his bread. My teachings present the teaching of spiritual leaders who lived at least 2,500 years ago, such as Fu Shi, Shen Nung, the Yellow Emperor, Chuan Suey (my ancestor), Niao, Shun and Yu. They were genuine social leaders of high spiritual quality. Their spiritual quality and their great contribution was recognized by people. My family is descended from the healer emperor Chuan Suey (2536-2436 B.C. reign), who was a grandson of the Yellow Emperor (2698-2598 B.C.). He was particularly noted for teaching people meditation and Chi Kung (Chi Gong) so that they could handle their diseases naturally.

When King Wen's son, King Wu, fought the tyrant Jou (1154-1125 B.C.), our ancestors could still produce a thousand chariots to join the revolution. The revolution was a success, so my ancestors shared part of the glory. They received titled land, and legally accepted residence as the County of Thousand Chariots in Sung Tung province.

However, at the end of the Chou Dynasty, we suddenly discovered that our way of life no longer fit into the mainstream of life; evil competition in all aspects of existence had begun. The peaceful golden era of the Chou dynasty (1122-256 B.C.) ended after 800 years; and the world, like a whirlwind, spun into the new direction that we live in today.

Regardless of the glory of yesteryear, the spiritual value of the Integral Way as the mainstream life spirit remains inviolate. The teaching of natural spiritual truth presents the spirit of the mainstream of life at all times, not the paltry path of religious escape.

I understand that there is a need for different spiritual practices for different kinds of people. Some people become nuns or monks, because it is a natural fact that they are only suited for that type of life. However, that does not mean that a cloistered life is suitable for all people. In the past, too many people living that way resulted in an unhealthy development in society. Today's society needs to restore a healthy life spirit as the fundamental direction for our lives.

Salvation is for people who are sick and weak in their life spirit. Spiritual faith is not an excuse for leaders to establish power over people. Neither is it an excuse for people to live irresponsible lives or to eat the fruit of other people's labor and hard work.

Religious leaders establish religion aside from the political establishment to share the special privileges of society, to be above the general populace and to eat its grain without being directly involved in the productivity which is the real strength that supports people's lives. This kind of negative teaching has existed for close to 2000 years or more. Shall we continue it, or shall we all wake up to find our natural life spirit? We need that spirit; otherwise our spirit will never be healthy as natural life. This is the foundation I offer and this is the contribution I would like to provide for our new future.

VI

We need to think about ourselves as a school of philosophy, a school of spiritual practice or a school of spiritual attitudes. Let us not think of ourselves, treat ourselves or develop ourselves as a religion. There are already too many religions with too few good results. By not being like a religion, we can remain objective and serviceable to whosoever needs help. We like to attract people who do not profess any religion, but we respect the faith of people who do, because it is their personal choice. If anybody who belongs to a religion comes to learn from you, they do not need to convert. Their own spiritual growth will lead them where they should be. We do not need to convert people to a new type of thought. New spiritual leaders, new church organizers and old churches also can adopt my teaching without the need to convert themselves.

This great task you have undertaken still needs support from all old religions, but our spiritual mission is different from theirs. Our mission is to bring about a new high civilization: that is, a world which has no war, a society which has no litigation, a world of love, a world of mutual concern and help where all people enjoy their lives, and where people are ready for self-reliance during difficult times. In such a community, there are no struggles between people, no riots, no strikes or mob protests. Such a society will be a world of peace, harmony and unity. This is what I think is worthy for us to pursue. The new high civilization depends on the spiritual development of people who can accept technology as the physical foundation for spiritual support.

Actually, the teaching of the Integral Truth is ageless. It prevails and is apparent at every moment, but people neglect it. People even neglect the common sense of a healthy natural life.

My talking about the attainment of spiritual sobriety may lead you to think that I am afraid of antagonizing religions. That is not the issue. The world needs help at all levels, including new cultural, philosophical and educational tools. Maybe people who need religious help will not find what they need if they come to us. What we can handle is people who approach normalcy; with some help, they can easily see and then conduct themselves on the right path.

The conventional religious approach is much stronger than what we do, so we have no competition from any religion. We are open; we offer service to whomsoever approaches us. We never manipulate others, but just offer what has been learned.

VII

Keep away from politics. Politics have a different function than spiritual help. Over the last 2,000 years, religions promoted many good ideas but could not get them accomplished. Those ideas were then accomplished politically, ideas such as social welfare and a common market. With that in mind, you may think that politics can be positive and beneficial, but I wish you would not become active politically. Instead, help the modern politicians with their spiritual development. Encourage the political leaders of far vision and foresight to accomplish the world as one nation and one government.

A little over 200 years ago, the first leaders of this new free country engendered a new political system based on a deep conviction in Heaven and God. They were looking for free expression and formation in the worship of God. Because they had a deeper understanding about what is right and wrong in politics, plus an ample share of good faith, the forefathers of the United States laid down a foundation which is still something to be proud of.

Nevertheless, during the last 200 years, much has changed. The leadership of this nation has also changed and is not as spiritual as before. There is not much spirit in politics. Regardless, the spiritual essence is the essence of all lives, so all of you have some responsibility to help political leaders have a correct understanding about the human spiritual direction.

If the president and the majority of Congress belonged to one party, they would create policies which favor that party. By overextending in one direction, their policies would later become a burden or mistake that stood in the way of a progressing society. My spiritual recommendation usually concentrates on individual spiritual self-cultivation. Yet whatever attainment is achieved on the level of general life will be blown away if society is not improved. Therefore, spiritual cultivation must be internal and external at the same time. When one wishes to attain spiritual development, one cannot ignore society because spiritual development is both internal and external, individual and social.

The world is too big to fulfill the great goal by the effort of only a few individuals. The self-government of each individual and each smaller community can easily be accomplished. At the same time, each individual and community cooperates with each other to achieve peace, harmony and prosperity in the world.

Each individual and small community is the foundation of a nation and of the world. Therefore, the principle of self-cultivation and self-government is the foundation of a healthy organic world. The entire world is actually one person or one being as an individual self.

Most people think that the source of violence in an individual or society is the stomach. In reality, violence is associated with sexual energy and sexual fantasy. Some people can comfortably adjust their sexual demands, but others cannot due either to natural reason or defect. Some people easily attract the opposite sex while others do not. An improvement for each individual would be to be harmoniously present with their life company without being sexually involved. That would also help prevent violent incidents from happening. It would be good for some individuals to engage in celibacy and live in a spiritual community such as those of ancient times in which single people pursued their spiritual purpose. Anyone who can transform the possible violence of their undissolved and unfulfilled excess sexual energy into social service and moral fulfillment performs a great service to the world.

I have pointed out that the goal of the world should be independence, liberty, justice, mutual help, security, universal love, no pressure, and no tension from hostility. How can this be achieved if men do not respect women or women do not know how to respect men? Each needs to accept the other's natural differences and not try to compete over them. A harmonized society cannot be achieved without the basic harmony between man and woman.

Q: Politics is one of the major tools which shape culture, and culture keeps us from the natural way. How should we get involved and how or what should we support politically?

Master Ni: Let me address this by giving an illustration. For example, you do not know what your own daughter's development will be. Maybe she will become involved in politics; good politicians are nurtured by the family. If you lay down good principles for her now, then we shall have a good political leader. Political leaders today are brought up in the street. They are not very different from a kind of gangster except they have better luck. We need to educate our future political leaders. The politicians now are too proud; they do not have time to listen to what you say, what you think and how deeply you have reached, because that is a different direction. What they want is money, votes and position; that is all.

With your help, step by step, we can let them recognize what is the right way to go and what is the wrong way to go. They are smart, they will understand, because they have a speculative nature like stock brokers. When society turns around, they like to position themselves as forerunners and spokespeople for what society already reflects.

Q: I understand the subtle cultivation of the new generation, but how can we be patient for the next ten or twenty years?

Master Ni: I will not give you twenty years. We will slowly talk about this more, and then we will have a discussion in which I will give you instruction.

VIII

I would like to express my relationship with all of you. I would like to remain as a friend to all of you, to all people of the twentieth century. You are the real messiahs of modern times. A messiah is a person who can help people. You may think you are not because you think you do not possess magic power, but as I see it, you can perform the great miracles. A modern messiah has no need to perform magic tricks. His or her power is the ability to not join in spreading the plague which is being spread through sexual contact, and to not join inhuman destructive wars. A modern messiah can choose to protect lives from such irresponsible dark behavior in a war. You are the real leaders of modern times and your good leadership can help the world move toward the direction of health and balance.

All mentors are equal, but you do need a coordinator or manager to carry out the details of spiritual cooperation. The structure of leadership among mentors will be suggested when the time comes. Your ideas about this will also be valued before the decision of how to coordinate the mentors is made. My vision is to apply the seven star system of rotating leadership. I, however, am not that type of leader. I would like to give you support, but never think of me as the leader of your group. I am your cheerleader. I am your spiritual friend; I offer you the raw material of my teaching. You are the leaders of society and of the world.

I would also like to point out the relationship of my family to my teaching. My two sons are already overloaded with work. They are very supportive of my work, but they are not leader types of people either. We would all like to give support in whatever area needs it. I will consider whatever support we can give as our contribution to the fulfillment of our personal life. In the real field of people, we know our limitation. We would like to assign the whole responsibility for the promotion of the new spiritual renaissance to all of you.

IX

I consider all of you like my sons and daughters. Once you are involved with the public, I would like you to remember the illustration I give you now. You know how water from a high mountain stream runs down to the river and then to the ocean? At the beginning, the running water in the stream is crystal clear and pure, but downstream you cannot see through it, because the water has become so murky. I would like all of you in your lifetime to maintain yourselves as clear, drinkable water just as you were in the beginning.

In order to do this, three things need to be avoided. First, do not look for power. Power can corrupt you. Instead, look for service.

Second, do not look for money. Do your job, and be supported by it, but do not be greedy. All of you who will become teachers and spiritual workers need to be able to concentrate and produce good work, so you need to be paid for your teaching and service. If you organize a center, it should be supported by the people who use it. All that does not bother me, but do not be greedy and fall into the money trap unless you have a good goal which requires money.

On this point, I will have great respect for you when your life and your spiritual work are self-supported or at least half self-supported, so that your work is a spiritual contribution and virtuous fulfillment. If you are going to concentrate on teaching, then I advise charging students fairly and correctly. You can also offer some free classes for youth who need to learn but have no money or allow people to make an affordable donation if they cannot pay full rate. If a good sum of money is received from donations, the money should mostly be used for developing the teaching to enable it to reach all people. The money policy can be determined after all practical needs have evolved.

Third, do not involve yourself in improper sexual relationships. Young men and women who are mentors are allowed to have one partner with whom they are together for a year or longer. The purpose of this is to force you to become more selective. Surely a normal marriage is preferred. Confused sexual relationships with many people is not suggested either for mentors or for students. As a mentor, you conduct a group of people. I suggest that you respect your position and your work. It is important for you to set a good example. I do not think sex is evil, but it is not suitable for someone who is supposed to be dedicated to the spiritual love of many people to irresponsibly indulge his or her sensual desires.

Mentors might consider choosing a partner who shares the same spiritual pursuit and who would be helpful in one's work. At least the person can give virtuous support without any deception that would affect one's concentration and devotion.

X

I would like to quote two sentences from the *Tao Teh Ching* connected with your work. Practically and firstly, we need to recognize that each person has individual desire, ambition and personal interest. You cannot totally deny this, because it is human, but it should not be over-encouraged. Communists talk about how evil capitalism is, but the communists cannot find sufficient initiative for people to go to work. When people go to work, they expect to have freedom and to be appropriately rewarded. That is human nature, and cannot be denied.

Honey bees go to a field and gather pollen from the flowers. Their honey is not produced for human use; it is for themselves. If the bees knew that their honey would be taken away by humans, they might become lazy or even refuse to work. In the human world, if everything is supported, and if everything belongs to everyone, then people naturally slow down to become equal with all other people. Thus, government promotion of a strong military nation is negative for the world's health because it does not bring goodness to people's lives. I would not unreasonably reject all systems of government, but we need the deep vision to understand the benefit and the disbenefit of each system.

Even bees know how to work hard; it is their natural instinct. They even produce more than enough honey so humans can share it. If a society does not disturb the natural human instinct for initiative and creativity, people will always create more, but mostly people can share prosperity together. These details come from observing human experiences which paid a price and which can serve as examples to warn us against doing anything that damages the organic condition of life.

There are two sayings of Lao Tzu which are especially appropriate to your work. Lao Tzu says, "When you do more for people, you get more." What does that mean? It means when you do more for others, then you also receive more. It means the development of all others contains your own development. You do not need to consider your personal gain; you shall be prosperous with all others.

The second saying of Lao Tzu is "The one who is selfless accomplishes the self." Truth is paradoxical but it is also useful in your spiritual life and in your practical life. The application of this saying means that if you become selfish, you become smaller in achievement. If you reach out in a small range, your gain is small. If you are selfless, your accomplishment is usually much greater. The wise teacher gave us this ageless life guidance.

Now I would like to restate or reconstruct Lao Tzu's sentence like this: "The one who helps the accomplishment of other people's lives also helps the accomplishment of one's own life," or "If you do good and nice things for people, in the end, you are not left out." I offer this advice as guidance for the life of all mentors.

XI

Originally, the Integral Way was the inheritance from ancient wise ones who were universal personalities. The Integral Way is derived from these books: *The Book of Changes and the Unchanging Truth*, the *Tao Teh Ching*, *Chuang Tzu*, the *Yellow Emperor's Internal Work*, and *Lieh Tzu*, who is quoted in *Tao, the Subtle Universal Law*. If you follow those books correctly, you can accomplish your life happily without becoming involved in the mayhem of different conceptual struggles. To learn the law of healthy conceptual management, you need only concentrate on practicing the guidance given by those books. In particular, I recommend the *Esoteric Tao Teh Ching*.

A fragrant plant naturally gives its fragrance without command or demand. I believe all of you are like fragrant trees or plants who naturally give out your fragrance. You are not poison oak or poison ivy. You are beautiful trees of life; you possess the fragrance of nature. Your fragrance is not used to deodorize somebody else's bad odor, but it makes the world a sweetly scented place to live. This is the spiritual function all of you can fulfill.

Q: If all of life is a balance of forces, is it ever possible for the world to become completely peaceful, without conflict and with total understanding and cooperation? What I mean is, if life has both its dark side and its light side, is it ever really possible to reach an ideal of equilibrium? Won't there always be a counterbalancing force that causes the demise of that ideal?

Master Ni: She is talking about yin/yang theory. We can apply that on a different level, but you still need to achieve unity between the two sides which are struggling. Otherwise, we could not live together. Strength comes from internal unity. When you face different challenges, challenges are what you like and where inspiration comes from. Badness is what inspires goodness.

This is fully discussed in the *Tao Teh Ching*. We need to attain internal strength. When you sail a boat in a strong wind, the boat goes this way and that. You have to skillfully handle your sailboat, otherwise it will turn over. We cannot totally avoid swinging to one side or another, but we manage a maximum of balance. That is the necessity. Living in the world is exactly the same as handling a sailboat: our internal strength must balance external worldly pressures to save ourselves from falling. In our lives, we like to enjoy all good things, but with internal strength and without falling.

For example, if you go to Disneyland, there are all kinds of rides. However, I do not think you could go on all of them in one day. You could not enjoy more, because you are not strong enough; you become tired by the end of the day. Let us have the strength to enjoy life but let us not be defeated by our enjoyments.

I believe that all of you have already become my spiritual friends, although physically some of us are new acquaintances. You probably know the world's trouble better than I do. I just pay enough attention to say there is a lot of trouble, but what is important is how we work it out. You cannot walk away, so how can you turn the situation around? Maybe you are interested in finding a new way.

I wish to offer a foundation or direction for working in the world. At different times or epochs, people's lives have different spiritual missions. If you understand that, I would like to ask you, why did you choose this time to be born? You could have come earlier or later. Actually, we still do not know if there will be a later in this world.

You had a reason for coming here, and you have come to this retreat because you have lost your purpose in the world. You have forgotten the original purpose of why you have been born at this time. For many years you have been drowning in the world's hot water. You might reach the shore, but there is no shore for you to reach unless you are spiritually achieved. If I allowed all of you to do a special 49-day meditation with lots of fasting, most of you would remember and know why you have come back here. However, I could not do that, because it would make you too weak, and you could no longer work for yourself or for the world again. This is why I just work to awaken your soul.

All of you have a good soul; all of you have a purpose in coming here to the retreat. You knew that somebody would be here to wake you up.

To save a lot of discussion, let us come to the point: I ask you, are you interested in helping yourself and helping the world or aren't you? If you are interested in helping the world, then how will you go about doing it? We do not need to bring anything from the spiritual world; everything is here. You have not yet discovered your potential. You are the strength to turn the world around.

Chapter 3

Light Speaks

The Time is Now

My beloved friends, although my teaching has been presented through quite a number of books, as mentors all of you shall carry the simple message from me which is contained in the following lines. As mentors, wherever you go, I wish you would read this oral teaching aloud and ask people to repeat it after you. My simple message is:

It is the time,
   the time is now.
It is now that you can
   return to the Integral Truth of life.
The fire of carnal life
   should be turned down.
The fire of spiritual awareness
   should be lit up.
You shall see the time is short.
The time is now.

It is the time,
   the time is now.
Those who glorify war will do so in vain;
   they will gain nothing but ruin.
Those who burn others' houses and destroy their fortunes
   will have their own houses burnt
   and fortunes destroyed.
Those who live an irresponsible life
   will destroy their own life,
   and damage the health of the world.

It is the time,
the time is now.
The earth is on the verge of vanishing.
God's will may change
because of the sincerity of the human heart.
The renewal of the human spirit could bring about
the last opportunity for salvation.

It is the time,
the time is now.
This is the last moment of sunset
for the old world,
Yet it is the dawn
of inner enlightenment.

It is the time,
the time is now.
The seed of your spiritual life
should be planted and grown.
It needs the great nutrition
and protection of the sky.
Everlasting life can only be found in people
who pursue spiritual immortality.

It is the time,
the time is now.
Respect our neighboring planets.
They are the territory
of great souls on earth.
The moon is the first station
for your landing.

It is the time,
  the time is now.
The moon was once a part of the earth.
It can only provide you with temporal safety.
It is the first station for your soul landing
  during a time of emergency.
All other planets and stars
  in the reachable range
  contain only the latent potency of life.
Yet earth is where flesh and soul meet each other.
This blessing of earthly life is unfortunately
  not recognized by most people.

It is the time,
  the time is now.
Most people with great souls
  can only reach the moon at will
  in the emergency of the troubled earth.
Only a highly achieved one
  enjoys the freedom to live in all the sky.

It is the time,
  the time is now.
Start your spiritual cultivation
  in order to nurture your everlasting spiritual life.

It is the time,
  the time is now.
By the light of the North Star
  your soul is guided to its heavenly home.
Even people who live in the southern hemisphere
  will reach the North Star
  by sincerity of mind.

It is the time,
  the time is now.
During your lifetime
  cleanse your soul
  of the sins you have committed.
Have you ever damaged your body,
  your mind or your soul?
That is what is called a sin.

It is the time,
  the time is now.
If you repent your sin secretly
  in daily purification,
  it only expresses your willingness in your prayer.
The most important fact
  is to change your life and your personality.
Sins can be removed by your new positive life
  which offers help to others
  with no motivation or thought of self.
Your sins can all be removed
  if you help hundreds and thousands of people
  move on the right path.

It is the time,
  the time is now.
Nurture your spirit.
Prepare your pilgrimage
  toward the North Star.
But to make it safe,
  your projection should be
  to Venus, Jupiter or Mercury.
With the help of the angels
  and all the immortal spirits
  your voyage will be safe.

It is the time,
the time is now.
Prepare yourself and others
by doing all the important steps.
Do not be hasty to leave your body
before you carefully cultivate your spiritual life.

It is the time,
the time is now.
All important sacred secrets
have been given to you.
Whatever you need to know and learn
can be found in my books.
Following the course charted for you
in truthful spiritual books
you can complete your spiritual self-cultivation.

It is the time,
the time is now.
Prepare your spiritual future
with utmost sincerity.
You will be rewarded by reaching the North Star.
There, with great joy,
you will meet your friends.

It is the time,
the time is now.
Lower the flame of your carnal fire.

Heighten the torch of righteousness
and spiritual unity of the world.
Following the light of the North Star,
you are safely protected
in your voyage through daily life.

It is the time,
the time is now.
The time is now,
now, now and now!

Q: When you mention the North Star, are you talking about something symbolic or do you mean the actual North Star?

Master Ni: It is not symbolic. Symbolic means your heart and your mind, but this time I am talking about the thing that is possible.

Q: Maybe I said the question backwards. Of what is the North Star a symbol? Other than a physical star, what is the meaning of the North Star. Or is there any?

Master Ni: We should have confidence that we have spirits. Do you know that in the vast universe there are angels and spirits? I have recently finished a book called *By the Light of the North Star: Cultivating Your Spiritual Life.* In that book, I recommend deep and serious meditation. Typically when people die, their soul goes out and they leave the body to disintegrate. Our cultivation is not that way; it promotes the union of the body and the spirit to produce a new life. It is a further evolution.

In modern life, most people do not even know which star is the North Star, but once you are out of the body there are two possibilities. If in your lifetime you are not prepared, you sink with your carnal desires, thus losing your freedom. In that case, there is no need to even talk about the North Star. The other possibility is that you can fly. If your soul is light, you will naturally fly without any traffic lights or policemen to tell you where you can go. The true traffic signal is in my poem; you should use it.

Once you achieve yourself, you will know that there is a different level of being than ordinary life. There are starry beings, heavenly beings, angels and all kinds of beings. Before you step out of your physical life, you only know that people all have nostrils, eyes, ears, etc. You cannot deny it, we all have the same physical shell. However, once you step out, how will you conduct yourself and where will you go? This book can give you some information about how to prepare yourself just in case.

During the last 2,000 years, many prophets have said that the earth shall reshape itself or vanish. If the earth vanished, what would all your hard work and strong interests mean to you? Then you come to the question: do you know you can save your own soul? My answer is yes, you can save your soul, because you have made the necessary preparation. The way to prepare yourself in an emergency is to go to the moon first.

Some people say that Los Angeles is not a good place to live, because of the threat of earthquakes. It is believed that someday the mountain range which runs along the middle of California will crack open and split the state into two parts, one falling into the ocean. If that kind of drastic disaster happens, how will you save your life? Will you yell? That will bring no help. Will you call the White House to come over to help? No, you prepare yourself ahead of time.

I am not using this example to threaten you. You can never assume that where you live on the earth will always be the same and always be safe. Do not trust it. I also do not need to threaten you by saying the time for that will come very soon. The reason I am sitting with you at this retreat today is because I have had no indication that tomorrow you will all be in water. With that kind of confidence, I am here. Otherwise, I would have sent you a postcard.

You know, such a thing can happen. It has happened before and it will happen in the future. This is why I am doing spiritual teaching, telling you to calm down and not rush around so much. Then before something happens, you will know about it and can prepare yourself. If you are too busy-minded and driving your car constantly on the highways, your nervous system will be too occupied to receive any message. Otherwise, why did ancient people do better than modern people? Even cats, rats, turtles, birds and ants know what will happen before an earthquake. But human beings talk a whole lot. Talk is noise. You can know ahead of time, surely you can know.

This kind of spiritual achievement is not the same as religious fervor. Religions are helpless unless you are able to center your energy. We still need to work and live our lives, but we also need to maintain spiritual centeredness so that when we are quiet, we can observe if something is wrong and know about it immediately.

In general life, please laugh. This teaching is nothing other than teaching people to laugh. That is important. When you aren't laughing, what do you do? You keep calm and quiet, and stay ready for the next laugh.

So the time is different. Although we can laugh, we still need to watch for what will happen in our surroundings. That is important.

To address your question, spiritually we often speak of the sun and moon metaphorically, but we do not usually talk about things in this deeper level. This description is more realistic than poetic. We have a lot of time to be poetic, but this matter is not poetic. When you have saved yourselves, you can write a two-line poem to me.

I think Dao and Mao have told you the other details of what you need for now, but this is my message to help prepare you. You know the direction I have pointed out already. Step-by-step, I will continue to clarify all of this. We can enjoy being anywhere, but at the same time, if the earth under your feet is dancing, and not only dancing but doing rock and roll, not only rock and roll, but doing a nosedive, you cannot dive with it. So prepare yourselves.

Q: Is the end or beginning of a millennium always a time of great change? At the turn of the last century we had the first World War. It was the last gasp of the aristocracy. After that, we went through a big transition.

Master Ni: Something similar or worse could happen. That was the era of the Wine God culture of expansion, colonialism, imperialism. All those types of thoughts, ideas and life attitudes cause the trouble. It is one's own life attitudes that cause trouble. They only bring death and destruction, because they are blind to what should happen naturally.

No one lives forever, but it is not right that anyone who lives here should spoil or destroy this place.

We have seen many great leaders such as Alexander, Napoleon and Genghis Kahn come along, fool around, make a lot of noise and then disappear. They did all irresponsible things in the world. Theirs is an unwholesome example that we need to change so that we do not continue to support similar leaders.

You can help develop a source of communication with the world. If not, then you can at least not join them; you have that strength.

Q: Do human upheavals in the world cause or have an effect on natural disasters or natural upheavals?

Master Ni: They also reflect the spiritual level. The human world shapes a spiritual reflection in the sky. Then a corresponding energy change will cause trouble, because the earth itself is a spirit. There is a lot of spiritual nature on earth; the earth is affected by individuals.

For instance, you might have a beautiful house, and maintain everything very well. One night when you go out your teenager, who enjoys rock and roll, invites all his friends over. When you come home, you feel differently; the energy is strange because it has been violated. I think world matters are more serious than the play of children.

That is a metaphoric example of how we make trouble. It happens because of the general lack of development.

Q: Does the source of spiritual energy that we are part of come from the North Star and then spread out to the surrounding planets? And when things happen on the earth, is the idea that we will go to the moon to collect ourselves and then proceed as an energy field toward the North Star? Will we be a united energy field? Does the trip take place quickly, instantaneously, or will there be a long time spent in traveling?

Master Ni: The angels, your true God, will tell you. At this time, we can only review a little bit, not too much. To discuss it any further would disturb too many people. They will say you are crazy to talk about this. We would rather people say you are of sound mind.

Q: Does the Book of Changes and the Unchanging Truth *offer the type of guidance we can use on a daily basis to prepare us for this coming situation?*

Master Ni: No. The *Book of Changes and the Unchanging Truth* only deals with your earthly activities. In the morning you might use the *I Ching* by asking, what is my energy today? Based on the indication of your energy situation, you might decide not to make investments or meet new people that day. You might go to a place where usually you do not go. If it is a good day, then you think good things will happen and you try to do something.

The *I Ching* is useful in reflecting your stage of energy, but spiritual cultivation is much deeper than that.

The *Book of Changes* is still the main book you can use to share with other people. Most people are not ready for you to go too deeply.

Q: What is the book you said that will help us prepare for our spiritual journey?

Master Ni: Last year, I wrote a few books which may help you. The *Esoteric Tao Teh Ching* can help organize your daily life and at the same time help your enduring life. Another book I wrote is called *The Way, the Truth and the Light*. That too can help you have another spiritual vision that goes into why we do not understand spiritual matters in the first place. It is a collection about spiritual vision. Then there is another book called *Immortal Wisdom*, which talks about immortality and soul projection. Many people are excited about astral projection, but that is not achievement. It is natural for people to project themselves when they die. They even project from time to time without knowing about it.

Then there is the book called *From Diversity to Unity: Spiritual Integration of the World.* The following book will be *By the Light of the North Star: Cultivating Your Spiritual Life.* These are all recent books. Some are still in the process of being printed. I wish you would pay attention to them.

You can also use the *Workbook for Spiritual Development of All People.* The invocations or incantations in it are not for the human level, they are for the level of natural energy and natural spirits to help you gain some power or authority if you are in some danger or if you are not used to the natural spiritual environment. I mean, if you go to a place and you do not know how to protect yourself. Those things are for your own protection. They have a real effect, because when I chose to translate them, I was careful about them. The point is how you issue or form your own subtle energy.

Anyone who is really interested in joining my work will find that it is simple. It does not mean that you have to establish yourself as a teacher, although you are surely welcome to do so. If you have enjoyed this message and would like to share this kind of awakening with others, then you can consider yourself a mentor. I do not think it is necessary to ask you one by one if you are interested in being a mentor, but I would like to hear your collective voices say "yes" or "nay." *(Everybody says yes.)*

Q: In the Workbook for Spiritual Development, *there are a lot of invocations that refer to the Jade Emperor. Can you explain who or what the Jade Emperor is?*

Master Ni: I have explained it in the book, *Tao, the Subtle Universal Law.* It is the most undecayable, refined energy of the world. You also have that energy. We are human people who have both a rough part and a refined part. It is not worth working hard for the rough part. We only use the rough part to carry the essential part.

In ancient times, many people competed to be emperor. However, all emperors must die, so being emperor was not the goal of the ancient developed ones. They valued what did not decay. They considered the undecaying essence of life, your life spirit, to be the Jade Emperor. Many people worship emperors for political reasons, but spiritual people worship the jade-like emperor who never decays. I consider this the humor of the ancient spiritually achieved ones, not a rigid establishment. However, folk Taoism makes it into a religion.

Jade has the property of preventing the decay of the body. When the Chinese nobles died, they put a piece of jade into their mouth and sewed pieces of nicely cut jade with gold thread into clothing. This was worn by the dead body to prevent decay of the corpse. Recent excavations have revealed corpses thousands of years old which are better preserved than modern corpses are by refrigeration.

These types of preservation are not respected by spiritually developed people, who respect the undecaying essence of life. They are not attached to bodily life. Although they respect the unity of life physically, mentally and spiritually, the most valuable thing to them is the undecaying life spirit which can form itself again and again with a flesh body.

Even if you are not rich and cannot afford gold and jade clothes or refrigeration, and no matter whether you are buried or burned, there is something that is not buryable or burnable or destroyable. That is your life spirit, the Jade Emperor of your life. We respect and value the Jade Emperor of all lives. We like to work for it and live for it. This is the Jade Emperor of you, of me, of everyone.

> *When the world is gone,*
> *you are not gone.*
> *When the world has not come,*
> *you are already there.*
> *You are the Great Jade Emperor.*
> *The Great Jade Emperor is with us all the time.*

Q: People have often asked me whether or not a person can change their energy. For example, if they focus their energy internally, are they actually moving energy or are they just imagining that they have moved the energy?

Master Ni: I think you are talking about moving your chi in meditation or in Tai Chi movement. You do feel the energy when it moves just beneath the skin. When it moves deep inside, then you do not feel it. However, that does not mean that your energy is not moving.

Such a thing can be commanded by your mind, but to allow nature to function by itself is best.

Chapter 4

Sky Speaks

Your Cultivation Connects with
The Better Survival of All People

I

Part of my work has been to offer the most important information for internal development. Yet, this is merely one approach to help the world. It is inadequate. Thus, I am asking for your hands, your minds and your energy so that we can work together for the realization of a new, higher civilization.

The task in front of us is to look for the everlasting survival of humankind. We are not trying to establish ourselves in the world. This task needs good leaders to come along who can produce selfless leadership. This task needs talented people to offer their management capability and organizational talents.

After such a task is accomplished and the world has been harmonized, I hope you will remember what I have said here. The name of the external structure or organized institution which carries out the work should disappear. At that time, you will probably need to physically or spiritually guide the voyagers or travellers to one of the constellations in the direction of 2 o'clock from the earth's axis. Until that time, reach for whatever support the old custom can give you. You need all the support you can get for the new civilization, but the name only needs to be maintained until the job is done. Your personal spiritual attainment will last forever. I am telling you not to model yourselves after religions.

My vision is that the first stage of work will last for 15 years, from September 1992 to September 2007. The goal of this period of work is to inform the world of the existence of such an effort. We would like to become recognized as a vehicle for reaching the goal. In order to reach such a goal, because there is more concentration there, I request those talented people in the Atlanta Center to prepare themselves to offer help in other places by setting up centers that will serve the world.

Each center can be organized by itself. If anyone needs technical assistance, they may contact the Atlanta center[1] for help with different details, guidelines and so forth on how to form the center. The direction of the work now needs to focus on the modern world, which is the western countries.

Where should you start to work? That answer will be given according to your request of spiritual response, because this work is the cooperation of the supreme realm of the immortals and human spirits like mine and yours. Set up a center that will offer all types of programs to help people become spiritually developed.

Recognize the crisis of the turning of the century from the past 2,000 years and consider it as the new beginning of the next 2,000 years. Be careful: create no threat but maintain your alertness. All of you need to strengthen your potential internal survival during this time when external survival is difficult.

As I see it, all strength for helping society must come from society itself. We would like to see everyone support this renaissance without attempting to establish their individual private interests. All tasks meet with challenges and difficulties. There may be misunderstanding or competition as you do your work, but look at any challenge or competition to see if it offers better leadership with real virtuous fulfillment. If it does, we should help them. We would rather be assistants or supporters rather than leaders. The Integral Way itself may sometime disappear and be absorbed by a new leading force.

The world belongs to everybody, not only you and me. Then why do we need to stand up to say, "Do this"? It is because we would like to attract higher talented people to come to be the leading personalities in the world. We like to work quietly as supporters, mostly for our own spiritual growth. The great goal can be accomplished by leaders who

---

[1]The Center for Taoist Arts, PO Box 1389, Alpharetta, GA 30239-1389.

come along. We do not need the name, the position or the benefit; we do not want to be a world religion. We want a new human society and high civilization where people can enjoy peace, safety and happiness.

In order to be able to freely enjoy the new, high civilization, our effort is to change and improve any language or poster, term or ritual which is not suitable for this important purpose, and adopt any good approach to help accomplish our spiritual mission.

We can not excuse ourselves from such a great challenge and task. I request your capability of management and organization to move toward such a goal without yielding. As the ancient spiritual developed one said, "Until I see the benefit for all human people, I will never yield my duty and responsibility to someone else."

I have given this great saying to all of you, my great helpers, to remember when you are rendering such service to the world as one harmonized society. Let us forever eliminate wars and any conceptual obstacles which have obstructed the unity and harmony of all humankind.

II

A number of students are here from the Center for Taoist Arts in Atlanta to be ordained as mentors. I will present the same message to you that I give to them, because I can see that all of you here are useful, helpful people. It would be better for anybody who would like for me to ordain them as a mentor to kneel or sit on the ground for better reception. It is not that I need you to bow.

It is important at this precious moment for me to formally give you this spiritual mission and spiritual support as I ordain you as mentors of the Natural Organic World.

The worldly purpose of my teaching was conceived 2,600 years ago. It is to see the whole world as one nation or as one big harmonious society. It is to see a society that offers the five great spiritual foundations of serenity, simplicity, natural development, peace and freedom from struggle with anything or anyone.

In my recent book, the *Esoteric Tao Teh Ching*, I recommend self-government to all individuals because so far, no single government has been capable of taking care of the world or its people. Even a good social policy or political administration cannot exist without creating a burden for people. The service given is small, but people usually carry the effects of corruption, ineffectiveness and uselessness on their shoulders.

Therefore, outwardly my teaching wishes that people would agree with the far-reaching vision of Lao Tzu which enjoys the great world and the great individual life of natural orderliness and organic function without internal worry or external pressure. My teaching also wishes that people could live without being harmed or suffer from negative restraints or be burdened by any artificial or unnatural social structure.

People of self-government can come together as the Society of Integral Wayfarers and realize this important goal among themselves while still adapting to external social customs of their time. A Society of Integral Wayfarers, through its healthy natural organic function, would provide an influence which may help the world turn around to enjoy the same far-reaching vision as Lao Tzu. This would be far better than any revolution.

The world goal of serenity, simplicity, natural development, peace and freedom from struggle should not be ignored. If this goal is understood and accepted, we can come together as truthful workers for such a unique opportunity for a better life. Whoever sympathizes with a Natural Organic World (which I call "NOW") does not need to convert any reasonable customs, faith, psychological structure or lifestyle to become a member of the Society of Integral Wayfarers.

This is the worldly goal of my teaching. I wish that all of you might become the mentors of such a Natural Organic World. I accept that all of you will become mentors; among you, there will be many good leaders. So far, I am your co-worker.

I need to clarify my relationship with all of you. Before, people called me Master Ni. I thought it was a western custom, so I tried to adapt to it, but now it is not necessary to follow custom. I would rather you call me "friend." There is no need for either a first name or a last name. The true traditional spirit is that one does the work but does not receive the name. Then how do people distinguish who is the ancient teacher? They used "Tzu" as in Lao Tzu, Chuang Tzu, Pao Po Tzu, etc. Tzu means son of man. However, because the conception of son of man has been used by a sage known to the West, I would rather be "friend."

I am a teacher of Tao, not a teacher of Taoism. Tao is something that never dies; it is continually unfolding. The difference between Taoism and Tao is that Taoism is like a dead fish which is cooked with spices and served on the table. Tao is like a fish in a river or ocean, today, tomorrow and all the time.

The teaching of Tao, which we also call the Integral Way, is an objective, scientific search for practical improvement. It is different from Taoism, which uses imagination to satisfy the imagination, achieving nothing one generation after another.

The teaching of Tao does not stop your imagination but keeps it alive. In contrast, Taoism is 'cooked' imagination; it is dead. It has no potential life of new creation.

The teaching of Tao is ageless. It is not limited by any age, place or people. On the other hand, Taoism has a tradition lasting only several hundred years and its traditional concepts have limited people's life potential.

The teaching of the Integral Way is unconventional. We are non-traditional because we need to keep our spirit of initiative alive. Our source is the earliest human spirit which was born into the world with two missions: 1) to overcome the physical need for survival, and 2) to overcome the internal animal spirits and nature in order to accomplish the standard of humankind, which is a transitional life being. These two things are accomplished in order to attain higher evolution and integration.

Tao is the spiritual root of all human people. In contrast, Taoism with all its sects was merely a spiritual reaction to a certain time in some small regions.

The title of Taoist Master does not accurately describe me as a teacher of natural or original life spirit. My teaching is the teaching of natural spiritual truth, the teaching of spiritual root, the teaching of the natural healthy way, the teaching of spiritual unity, the teaching of spiritual integration and sublimation, the teaching of the Integral Way, the teaching of balanced centeredness, the teaching of the ageless truth and the teaching of the original Tao. I am the teacher of what I have described here, not a master of self-presumption. I do not enjoy that type of mastery.

Our work is not a personal or individual promotion. Our promotion is the New High Civilization, the Natural Organic World, the Integral Way, but not any individual. However, I respect anybody who offers leader energy, who is efficient in managing and in organizing work and people. Such people should be recognized and credited. I do not need any decoration, because I truly recognize that the highest leadership is the Universal, Everlasting Spirit of Life. It can be any of us, or anybody who expresses the most healthy, most harmonious and most selfless natural virtue. If you recognize its leadership, you recognize all those others and myself as your friend.

From now on, if some of you call me Master Ni from habit, I will not be upset. For most of you, if you accept the Universal, Eternal, Most Healthy, Most Harmonious, and Most Righteous Spirit of Life, it is not a bother whether I have a name or not. My work is not purposely to establish a name in the West or East among any generation of human people. I only trust myself as one element of this universal life.

I will greatly appreciate whatever help you give to the work of human spiritual awakening among all people. In the past, public or social service has ben ruled by the star system like Hollywood advertisements which use a person's name to promote a project. I would like to change that. No individual name is to be promoted, but only the Integral Truth of life.

The time is now. The pioneers of this vision have been bystanders for 2,500 years wishing for the opportunity to turn the world around to the Way. Now is the time. I do not encourage you to escape as did the old type of spiritual practitioners who retreated from the world. I encourage your clear vision and principle of such a society. This has been expounded in my book, *Life and Teachings of Two Immortals, Volume II: Master Chen Tuan* and in my other books.

III
Ordination by Universal Conscience

I recognize your spiritual quality. When you go in to the field of work, you shall meet difficulties and challenges. Do not be discouraged or frustrated by these because they are opportunities for growth. First of all, you can meditate on the problem or question; then you will get an answer. Keep the answer for a number of days, or at least for over 24 hours or until after you have rested. After you receive your answer, if you need to find a unified way to handle a problem, consult with your fellow mentors and receive advice from the senior mentors. Practically, the immortal spirits work with anyone who is sincere.

In other words, your training starts when you become a mentor or start teaching. When you do your teaching you will be close to me spiritually, so you will be trained and supported. The authority to teach comes from your sincerity in learning and in achieving. Authority does not come from your skin color or birthplace. The people whom you help will not be attached to external appearances as long as you make yourself internally and externally unified as a devotee of this great task.

Your authority is determined by your own spiritual quality and sincerity in helping others, not by how long you have been with a teacher. A donkey that has been with its master for ten years is still a donkey. It may not even be a master donkey.

We live in modern times. I am proud of you who have gone through all types of education for many years but have not forgotten your spiritual purpose in life. Although you have not been with me long, I would give authorization to you, because I think you are truthful and trustworthy. I would not give authorization to a donkey, no matter how long it had been around a teacher.

You do not need to be born as a god. You do not need to be born from parents who were in the lineage of a certain spiritual tradition. You do not need to depend on any title to do this work. Just go to work as the conscience of society and humankind. Since this is a renaissance of the modern world, the highly developed, native inhabitants of any country have the authorization of their own spiritual duty.

Live a disciplined life and have truthful motives and correct approaches to helping the world; that is the qualification that is needed. The piece of stone that has been on my desk for the past 15 years as a paperweight and the silk flowers that have been in my house for many years are not transformed into something new or better by the mere virtue of their seniority.

Your great work will be appreciated by me. Keep yourself steady and make progress naturally. Enjoy the help that you give to the world and enjoy your own personal life. I require no sacrifice, but I do require you to set a good example.

Jesus is a great model of spiritual work for all of us. I only require you to be 50% like Jesus; by this I mean, work for the world but do not die for it. I want you to learn to live and laugh. Your laughter can break through all the riddles of theology. With your sincere dedication, the world will be peaceful and healthy and in good order.

Jesus was not understood; he was portrayed as a victim by generations of ambitious people, but the people who sincerely accepted his model were respectable, just as your life at the present time is also respectable. Each of you are messiahs in the modern world, but remember that Jesus is still a spiritual model for all of you, and the messiah spirits of Jesus still live within you.

Now, with the spiritual vision and mission of Fu Shi, Shen Nung, Yellow Emperor, Niao, Shun, Yu, Lao Tzu and other sages, I ordain you as mentors for the Natural Organic World.

Chapter 5

Wind Speaks

The talk in this chapter was given on September 6, 1992, the second day of the Annual Retreat of Yo San University of Traditional Chinese Medicine in Santa Monica, California.

The World's Trouble Needs to be Worked Out
By All of You

I

I make friends mostly through my writing and my practical work, so now I would like to introduce some friends who have come from Atlanta. They have come because they wish to do something to help the world and to help all of us enjoy ourselves.

We learn together and grow together. I greatly appreciate that they have come and we can all be together. I have given them a special assignment of being coordinators. If anyone in the future has an individual problem, or wishes to set up a center or start a group, please contact them; they will give you practical advice based on their experience. They might also assist you with some teaching duties. This is why I am specially introducing them.

Yesterday we gave your minds some stimulation. I hope and believe that you can understand what I see, which is not represented totally by my incomplete, special English. I do not ask for any immediate comments, but if you have any thoughts or ideas, we can discuss them.

As individuals, we struggle. This is why we come together as a group. We need to join our efforts. No individual is fortunate enough or strong enough alone, but working together, gathered together, we can be. As a group we are intelligent enough and spiritual enough to effect change. This is the benefit; we must use it.

Now, as we begin this meeting, I wish you would give me something to stir up everyone's morning mind. Usually the morning mind is slow.

Q: You mentioned yesterday that we could start thinking of ourselves as a school of philosophy or school of spiritual practice. Is the philosophical name something that you just use to help the public understand what you are doing or are you talking about helping people to use the intellectual mind to reach the truth?

Master Ni: Spiritually and intellectually, people reach me everywhere. I go everywhere, and once they know who I am, they come along. They say, "I use your book in my business and in training people for business." Or they say they use my teaching to help their clients and patients. My work has already been widely adopted. *The Book of Changes* is popular in foreign countries, not only in American society. Culturally, I have done enough. However, on the other hand, because the book distribution and promotion is not strong enough, we have further to go. As for how much we have reached people, we are doing quite well.

I would like to give you an encouraging example. Someone told me that several months ago some Russian people came to our clinic wishing to see me. They were so happy to see all the books. In Russia, for ten years or more they had one copy of *Tao, the Subtle Law* and they reproduced it on a copy machine. The book was in very bad condition from having been copied so many times. Just that one book came to their country, but they made copies so that a whole group of friends could receive and enjoy it. I feel encouraged by this type of work. People have a need for it, especially after having suffered so long under wrongful education which denies the spiritual aspects of life. That book, which is the product of a thousand or a million years of human experience, provided essential teaching, and the people who received it knew that it was right for them.

My writing is easily received by you because the truth is not only my truth, but your truth too. This book is not only my book, but it is your book too. I was born into a tradition of many achieved teachers who taught that first you learn, and then you go out into the world. This is what I did, and this is how I made friends.

The other day I talked with a student about the nature of God. I believe that in western or Chinese religious conception, Lao Tzu must be God, because he lived so long. A conservative historian estimated that he lived for 160 years, but another source believed that he lived for 200 years. According to the dates of his dynasty service, the change of sovereigns, he might have lived to be 500 or 600 years old. Physically, we do not have proof of that, and truthfully it does not really matter if he was physically old or not; his development was important. At that time, language itself was not well developed, yet he produced the book. I would like to ask you, at that time, who else had that much development?

There are people who develop as people, but maybe there are some people who still live like animals internally. Even in modern times, we cannot totally understand what Lao Tzu taught. How could he be more advanced than people who live in the modern 20th century? Yet the appreciation of him is so great that everybody still translates his work. They each like to twist his words a little bit to fit their own life experience, but that is all right, because it does not damage the content.

So anything you do is okay. You can organize a center differently, and as long as you associate or affiliate with your friend, Ni, Hua-Ching's teaching. I recognize your spiritual quality. The Chinese government wanted to send 1000 or more so-called Taoist priests to come over here to help me, but I do not need them. I need you to be the teachers and leaders of this society because I respect your mentality. The mentality of East and West is different. The Eastern mentality is good in certain individuals; in India, for example, the sages are highly developed, but if you go to the streets, you may be robbed, cheated or pick-pocketed. China was also a country with many developed individuals, but when the Chinese people come together, they cannot work together. When they come together, they are uncooperative and jealous, "You do better, so that means I am doing poorly." With an attitude like that, no progress or achievement can ever be made.

We need each individual's help. All people can learn the value of cooperation. For example, when I write a book, first I write or dictate. Then my helper types it out, and the material is returned with questions, "What does this mean, what does that mean?" I have to be patient and rewrite the English. Then there are fewer or no more questions at this stage. Then the material is sent out to a number of helpful people for proofreading and correction. Then I need to go back to another group of people to consult about the title or name. In the whole process, I have to be open to all questions and suggestions since I am working for the world, not for personal enjoyment.

I wrote a book about a famous sage who is widely recognized in the West. I called the book *The Clear Light of the World.* Then someone made a suggestion from the inspiration of his or her mother, whom I never met. The mother had lots of religious experience, and she said, this book should be called *The Way, the Truth and the Light.* I accepted. Spiritually, we need help from all developed people who can give support. We should recognize this ageless truth.

At the New Year celebration, people used to sit stiffly in the shrine while I wore a blue robe and did the service. It was not that comfortable. Anything I can do to get my message across so I can serve you better is the correct approach. We need a new approach for a new time. Who can offer this kind of wisdom so that everyone can apply it in their life?

Some people told me that they think I have a knack for using simple English to express different meanings, but I still feel that some English speaking people do not understand the phrase "The Integral Way." This is why I also call it "the Omni-Present Truth." It means that the truth is not only in places where sages were born or places considered as conventional holy lands. Truth is everywhere: in you, in your family, everywhere you can see the Omni-Present Truth. Then somebody said this was no good, I needed to find a better expression to tell the truth. In English, you have the word "immanent," which means "everywhere" or "indwelling," so I called it the Immanent Truth. Then somebody said that nobody knows the word immanent. What is truth? The truth is always truth, the simple Integral Way. Whatever suggestions you offer may be of benefit. That is no problem, but your questions are welcomed.

Q: What guidance can you offer sincere students whose spouse or family are involved in a different tradition or who do not appreciate these teachings?

Master Ni: We need to use an educational approach. We never use a policeman approach. Right or wrong, you cannot do that. You have to have patience. It cannot be done through intentional communication or everybody becomes very hot under the collar. You can occasionally give them some small unpurposeful communication and they become open. They need education. Why does the world, the family and the society have so much trouble? Because not even a good thing can be conveyed to them. Thus, we try that approach.

Q: Can you offer some guidance for raising children to learn the natural truth?

Master Ni: If you do not really have any interest in raising children, you had better not do it. If you are really more interested in playing the Chinese game called ma jiang, and a good card is more important than your own children, then how can you raise good children? If you do not feel happy, and do not really have the interest to raise children, then do not have children.

If you raise children, do not over-watch them, because each person born into the world has a personal nature to grow. In our own lives, we do not pay special attention to our stomach or our heart unless it causes us trouble. Children are natural lives and will grow by themselves.

You first need to train your children. When a boy or girl has a concept of money, you can start to train them to be frugal. When you give them money, you cannot act like some Chinese parents who enjoy playing ma jiang with friends all day and all night. If they are playing and the children ask for something, they say, "Okay take ten dollars and go away." What can you expect from those children? A person who grows up with some financial difficulty will manage money better and appreciate his life better. Some people complain, "I suffered when I was young from my parents' discipline or bad attitudes. My parents overdid it." I say, it does not matter how hard your life is, what is important is that you receive the lesson necessary for a positive contribution to your life.

Children are willful. They have no reason. What they want, they just want with no arguments. You need to learn how to transform their will into rational expression. If it is not transformed, then you are basically letting them stay at the stage of saying, "Father, give me a hundred dollars," and keeping it up until you give in. You need to guide them with a different approach: "If you do this, you shall receive the money." This is to say, if you do the right thing, you receive the reward. This is different, this is training, an educational process. You do it to help them not suffer in the future.

When I was a child, I wanted to buy everything I saw. I came back and begged my mother to buy things for me. She said, "You can do this and this," and that made me forget what I wanted, so every day I got one penny, then two pennies, not as a regular payment, but as a reward.

When I tried to make Maoshing and Daoshing do meditation, I would pay them fifty cents for one sitting. Maoshing did it a few times, then he forgot about it; neither of them liked to do it. Then I told my sons, you recite this short, four line poem, and the money is yours. If you make them desire to do it, then they will do it. The payment must be appropriate for the labor time they put into it. You need to redirect their willpower into a more useful form.

The truth is that, even now that we are adults, our achievement in life is the practical transformation of our own willfulness. Do you believe it or not? We just turn it around, because we have become more reasonable. It is not like going to your mommy and daddy and getting whatever you demand.

I would like to teach you a secret of happy life: watch what you want. You are happy to do what you like to do, so do it, and then let the reward come to your life without anxiety. In that way, you will be much happier. Some people might say, now I am 35, I have to own a four-bedroom house with a swimming pool and a garden. You better not think that way, because that will cause you frustration. That is external. It is more important to maintain your internal balance. If those things are good for you, and if the time is right, then naturally you can achieve it. But if something is not good for you, do not do it. For example, do you really know if having a big house is good for you, or if having a swimming pool is good for you? Those things all need lots of maintenance. I do not say that each of you should be as rich as someone who recently ran for the American presidency. I do not want you to be that rich, because there is no purpose to it. If you have a good purpose, then I would like you to be rich; you will become rich naturally. You might not have the same amount that the wealthy gentleman has, but you might be much more useful to people than he is. None of you is less than him; all people can enjoy themselves and be happy as long as they are not too emotional. If you are too emotional, sometimes you give yourself trouble. When you cannot control yourself any more, your emotion is an unpredictable storm.

Start low, do not seek reward, but do your job. Enjoy the things you do, and let nature bring about the rest. For example, in the fine arts market, one piece of art sells for big money. Do you know who enjoys the money? Not the artist; the artist only enjoys creating the art, and that makes their soul immortal. We have to learn one thing: do whatever is a good thing to do, even if you do not know if you will receive a reward or not. Forget about the reward. You should think, "I only do the things that I think are right, and that fit my life expression."

My friends help me do spiritual teaching, and they develop and promote goodwill toward one another. You may not be paid for your great work, but your purpose is serious. It is not like the Chinese amateur actors. In China there are many operas everywhere. If an amateur knows acting and would like to act on the stage, he or she will have to pay money to participate in the show for fun. Why? Because it is for enjoyment. Professional actors and actresses charge you, because they have to support themselves; happy or not happy, they have to do it. The amateur only does it because he or she is happy about it. You have to learn to do what you like to do. If you do not feel happy about doing something, then do not do it.

If you give me a birth chart, and if I have time, I can check out what financial attitudes your children will have. That is already determined, but you had better still train them well at the start and not spoil them. Give the right things to them.

Q: I have a lot of concerns about teenagers and their feeling that they do not have a future, as well as eating disorders such as anorexia and bulimia, and suicide. How can we help them?

Master Ni: There are two spheres. One way, I am not sure will help, because it is not necessarily available, but I will talk about it. If available, first you need to look for different types of foreknowledge. For example, if you have a good fortune teller who can tell the child what way to develop himself or herself, the child can know his own direction.

We were children once ourselves. You did not necessarily do better when you were a child than you do now, because each person has a cycle. If the children have no confidence, or have an eating disorder, etc. maybe they are in the time of a low cycle, and do not even know what they are interested in. Also they do not know how to develop themselves; it takes patience to show them. Even if you do not have access to a good fortune telling system, you still can understand a child, from the face and mentality. Each person has a mentality; the mentality has a shape, which can be subtly observed. The tendency can be observed. For example, if a child is picky in eating, then the child will not grow to be strong physically. If a child eats well, then he will become stronger physically.

So you first decide if this is a mental type of person or a physical type of person. However, you still need to be open, because each stage of development is different; then you can help them develop what they need.

Usually we can only set a good example as a father and a mother. Although they experience different stages of growth, they pay attention to your example. Even if you do not say anything, they still feel, "I should become like this, because my mom did this a certain way." Wordless, non-verbal teaching is more important than strong direct interference.

Q: Krishnamurti, who was an Indian sage, said that there is no such thing as evolution. I just find it interesting because he brought up his observation that sages come and go, and the students of a sage continually build up an organization around the sage, but no one really seems to achieve the same level as the sage. What do you think about that?

Master Ni: That is a personal definition of a sage. I will quote a Chinese proverb to you. There was a wise man called Chu Ku Liang, who was military advisor to the king. He gave great help to the king because he was a virtuous person. Just before the king died, the king held his hand and said to him, "You are a talented person; you have helped me greatly. You know my son is not good enough. Now I am finished. In the future, if you can help my son, please do so. If my son is really unworthy, help yourself and take over the kingdom." However, this man never took over the kingdom; he chose to help the lousy son. After 20 or 30 years he became old and weak, but he still took the army far out using the strategy of attacking border lands for the purpose of defense. The defense strategy was to continually disturb the border countries, so they would not have time to set up a big plan to invade your country. He died on the battlefield, exhausted. He was a gentleman scholar. Historically he was a great person, and everybody thought he was wise, so he became respected as a legendary figure. People thought he knew everything; practically, he was a faithful, wise person.

After he died, the son of the king who was the new king, surrendered to a border country's king. The border king give him a position with a useless title, several beautiful women and good food, and made him captive in some palace. What did he say to his close friends? "I am happy here; it doesn't matter if I am emperor or not. I am satisfied to be a captive with good women." I think all men would like that, but unfortunately he did not help the world much. Chu Ku Liang was wise. I have written about him in the *Book of Changes and the Unchanging Truth.* There you can find more about his story.

In China, we do not think that a cobbler has much wisdom, because making or repairing shoes is a small occupation. We have a saying, "If three cobblers come together, their wisdom might be sharper than the famous Chu Ku Liang." A sage is recognized as a sage, but it is always ordinary people who help the sage accomplish his plan. The credit belongs to the cooperation, not any single person, as I see it. In history, many great conquerors made names for themselves. Each had a great number of soldiers and generals who fought the war together with him. The heroic accomplishment was done by all, not by one person alone. A true integral sage does not make himself a sage. He would rather make his associates, students or friends into sages to accomplish the world together.

The *Tao Teh Ching* contains a different teaching than Krishnamurti's. I believe Krishnamurti was a good person and a good teacher. When he was young, someone used him by saying he was a messiah. However, once he grew up and became himself, he disbanded the order and did what he could by himself. There were two things that Krishnamurti did not achieve. One was to be a real messiah, and the other was to organize his force in a conventional way. I think he was wise.

Basically, I appreciate all pioneers of the new age who worked for the world before me or at the same time I live. Krishnamurti, Rajneesh, Yogananda, etc., have all passed away. They did something to open up western society to see the new light and pave the road for the future. No real sage can decide or insist, "I am the sage, and I have to do the job." A sage is a great student who can recognize advantages for other people and inspire new people to come together and accomplish a great work. For example, a general or great conqueror takes a whole group of strong men whom he can use as a stepladder so he can climb above them. A real sage is not that type of leader. I do not admire that type of world-blood-earthly leadership. I admire a person who does a good job without giving their name. This type of service is greatly appreciated.

We are supported by our spiritual background. Do you know your spiritual background? You cannot describe it. In your good life, any attainment from your spiritual development or growth is supported by your many good and bad experiences. Then you come to the point where you understand and appreciate the teaching. How can you decide that one single person is a sage?

We need to alter our hero worship to become the worship of really good spiritual qualities. Some people practice self-denial, such as not living in the world or doing anything for themselves, etc., but that is negative. There are others who deny their personal ego: I would like to help, I would like to do the things that I worship.

You have to know there are two traditions in China. One is the popular form of worship with colorful temples, statues and ceremonies. The other type is followed by people of high moral sense and is unknown to the general public. Real spiritual practitioners are called students or practitioners of the Integral Truth, or Shien Tao (the Union of Tao and People), which means an individual person is the complete universe.

In my books, I recommend Lao Tzu, Chuang Tzu, Hui Neng, Kou Hong and Chen Tuan, but I recommend them as individuals, not as a religion. A religion is a whole package. People can make a religion. You can also make a religion, but I would rather see you exercise your mind to use the inspirations of the ancient achieved ones to guide yourself to return to the creative source and unite with all. Hero worship is different than selfless service. A real hero can be found in the reality of everyday life, but he or she or the group receives no name.

So we would like to change the conception that any American president can fight a war for us. It is done by the enthusiastic people who come together to accomplish the same goal. We do not need to do things in the old way of party politics. You know, you can learn from your opponents. Maybe you can learn more from them than from your buddies. Maybe your friend is your enemy!

Do you consider me a hero? Maybe in the performance of this play, I am a hero. You know, Daoshing works, Maoshing works, and everybody here helps. Even in a small job such as a seminar like this, the real hero is not me standing here, the real hero is all the men and women who help put this thing together. You only enjoy the show, but I have lots of respect for every one behind the scene. In my work, I am quick tempered with those who help me to write. Sometimes I scold people when they do not understand. Then I have to explain; I need lots of strength to subdue my temper to tell the simple story over again and again to make people understand. You do not know how many tears and how much sweat has been shed by my helpers; they are the real heroes, not me.

In the future, our work attitudes have to recognize that no one person can do the job. We know that the presidents of American companies are very highly paid. What I do is actually fulfilling my life; I have a happy life. I do not need to follow the example of the C.E.O. of a Fortune 500 company who is paid more than all his workers. If that were my standard, I would become a person of no real 'income.' My real income is your good virtue and the friendliness you give to me. That is my earning. I am happy about that.

Q: Yesterday you mentioned the time period from September 1992 to 2007. Could you give us more information about that, what we can expect or anything you want to share?

Master Ni: Personally I would only give you four years to receive my spiritual inspiration, but I give you more, because my worker students are all slower than I am. I do not mind whether you achieve the world's goal I described, but I am happy to have you here.

Q: One of the things I appreciate about the teaching of the Integral Way is not only does it have the core Eastern teachings of emptiness and the self, but also the levels of taking care of yourself, your community and your family. It seems to include the whole spectrum, but it is so much, it is hard to know how to practice.

Master Ni: Wow, so simple! The following is one chapter of my new book. I will have my friend read it for you, then we will see its conclusion about the integral life. The integral life includes operating our own religion, our own company, our own bank - everything.

II
Frank Gibson reads Master Ni's written message which is written in a question and answer format.

Q: Master Ni, you always say spiritual life and secular life should come together. Would you please say something about politics and religion?

Master Ni: Surely, we can look deeply into the nature of politics, government, religion and spiritual learning.

In the past two thousand years of human history, in different societies of the world, religions have been used as the right arm of government. World leaders have abused military power, but they also know that military power is not enough to control people. There are too many "smart" people, so governments have supported religion, which has promoted different fears of the sky. Once people are subservient to their religion, then the religion supports the government in ruling the people.

Many people who came to the United States were people suffering from religious suppression. They came here to enjoy freedom of worship and spiritual practice. Many of those people were spiritual people.

The democratic political system was set up by the forefathers of the United States who were the leaders of their society. They came from a conventional society. They knew the shortcomings of the old system, and they wanted to produce a new one according to their understanding, life experience and knowledge. That group of people was developed enough to put together a government of conjoint ruling called democracy, which included freedom of religion. Democracy's foundation is that each person has self-government. People of self-government come together as a joined government; that is called a democracy.

Politics is a practical sphere of life. In a democracy, people come together to make a rule and everybody agrees on it. The foundation of the democratic political system is the consent of the people; it is agreement. If there is no agreement, there is no rule.

More than two hundred years have passed since the forefathers established the new nation, and American people work hard to promote American style democracy everywhere. Do today's leaders have self-government as individuals? Self-government means that people can govern themselves well and treat others correctly.

It seems that today's leaders lack that foundation. First, few modern leaders know the pure spiritual essence which exists above different religions; they are not even religious, period. Second, people have no depth of world

knowledge or world experience which makes them appreciate freedom and liberty as being almost as precious as life
itself. They do not know how to conduct their lives to enjoy
the fruit of the liberty and freedom they have been given.

Do people respect and value their freedom? Do they
also value the freedom of others? Do they respect their own
liberty? Do today's people have the same standard of
consciousness as their ancestors? When people are the
passive subjects of the ruling government, governments do
not do good things for people.

I think most people lack a strong commitment to the
health of society. If people who know the difference
between right and wrong lack a sense of responsibility, then
the spiritual quality of society is worm eaten. It is people's
responsibility to develop their knowledge of the difference
between right and wrong, so that the spiritual quality of
society can be protected and improved.

Q: How about science versus religion?

Master Ni: In the West, Christianity has fallen into decay
and internal corruption, which is a greater threat than
modern scientific achievement. With scientific achievement, people realize that there is no evidence of an awe-
some God, there is only blatant religious obligation which
does nothing to improve the life of society or of individuals,
but serves only the church itself.

Christianity did not suffer externally from people's
intellectual growth. Religions do face the pressure of
scientific achievement in holding onto the type of spiritual
vision as they promote, but the real pressure that is faced
by religions is mostly their own internal corruption.

Normally, scientific achievement is not evil except when
destructive weapons are developed. Normally, the purpose
of scientific achievement is to improve people's lives,
including their health. Good science also helps improve all
other aspects of people's lives.

Christianity was originally the essence of the western
world; at least it was the cultural pillar or cultural support

of western society. However, with the positive intellectual development of most people, Christianity or any other religion cannot maintain its position as part of the ruling force which makes God into an external power. Religions then cease to respect God as internal or spiritual, and as something connected with one's own individual spiritual self.

Q: What is the individual spiritual self?

Master Ni: Each person has an individual spiritual self. After developing oneself spiritually, each individual is God. When the spiritual selves of many people come together, we call this the common spiritual self, or God. Otherwise, you push your God too far away and make it unreachable.

There are two stages related to developing the spiritual self. In the first stage, you do not know that you have a spiritual self. The spiritual self functions spiritually to maintain your wholeness. In the second stage, your developed spiritual self is the fruit of your spiritual development. Does your spiritual self need development?

Again, when spiritually developed individuals come together, there is a common spiritual self, as God. Both the individual spiritual self and the common spiritual self need development and correct spiritual leadership, both internally and externally.

Q: In this society, we have already separated the function of religion and government. Is that separation correct?

Master Ni: The democratic system advocated allowing for the separation of government and religion. That is correct; let religion be religion, and let government be government. The reality is that when government and religion were connected, they took the life fruit from people.

Today, however, because people are allowed to have freedom, there are two things to do: one is to pay tax to the government and the other is to tithe the church, so that some day your soul will be saved. Government and religion still take and divide the booty of society. I would like to see the church help build good character in government. First, however, the church needs to regain moral discipline itself. That is the key to social improvement.

Q: What are possible sources of trouble in a democratic government?

Master Ni: A democratic government has two main branches: the executive branch and the representative branch for counter-balance, but positive cooperation can be obstructed under such a situation. Bad things cannot be done, but neither can good things be done by either of the two sides.

In a democratic government, the president belongs to one party. Sometimes the members of congress belong to another party, although that does not happen all the time. The president and the congress do not always work together for the goal of improving people's lives; instead, they fight for the political benefit of their own party.

Let me tell you how they divide the booty. When one party has something to be accepted by the other party, the other party needs something in their favor to be accepted by other side. It is an unwritten custom that such trade and exchange happens all the time in the government.

Public servants need to pick the policies which can serve our nation best. However, by dividing the political benefit for each side, this government will guide society nowhere. The result of economic failure, which is the national debt, is obviously the result of compromises between the two parties. No one can say which side must take more responsibility for it. Their only principle is the negotiations which occur under the table, compromising and dividing the booty. The whole system is corrupt under the principle that if you want me to agree with you, you must give me something in exchange. Such a political direction does not look at the true need of our people.

On the platform, politicians may sound convincing, but when they are elected to office, they are unable to accomplish their stated goal. There is only a limited arena for exercising their goodwill. They need to nurture their vision of worldly spiritual or moral problems rather than spend all of their time raising money to be re-elected. The spiritual improvement of society as a whole is the direction of my work, which needs more good, talented leaders.

This world is everybody's world. A nation is everybody's nation, and a government is everybody's government. A politician's support should not depend upon how well he or she can gather money or please the masses. If that is all they do, there is always a great distance from moral principles.

No doubt everybody has rights. No school or religion teaches everybody's rights, everybody's discipline, or everybody's sense of morality. Instead, religions talk about money; if you give me money, I will take your soul to Heaven. Truthfully, politicians and preachers are just people, and all people need a good spiritual education of the right way to live.

Q: Master Ni, we have lost confidence in churches. What is the other choice?

Master Ni: I advocate individual spiritual learning more than any single religion or church. For me, it is more important than just describing the unhealthy side of culture. My position is to give you a spiritual warning. A number of years ago, there was a church called the People's Temple Sect in San Francisco. About 700 or 750 people in this group moved to South America. Out of spiritual immaturity and disappointment in the political system, and because they killed a senator who made an investigation there, they all ended their lives. For a long time they prepared the poison to kill themselves. After that, in the United States, the parents of any family with youngsters interested in spiritual study were afraid of trouble.

In the spiritual heritage of the Integral Way, people always learn individual spiritual independence. Spiritual development is your own business. Surely people can learn together and be together, yet spiritually each individual is independent.

In this society people talk about democracy. However, the most suitable religious or spiritual teaching is not to accept rulership. Surely we value the correct management of the government. However, in your own life, the government is not the ruler, you are. Most of all, each individual needs to achieve one's own spiritual independence, especially people in positions of leadership. Leaders should not be influenced by other people; then they will be morally strong enough to carry out what is right for all people.

Q: Master Ni, what is more important, politics or living a natural life?

Master Ni: Society, government and religion are all important aspects of external life.

What is the guidance we have received from ancient times about the natural healthy way of life? The *Book of Changes and the Unchanging Truth*, states that a leader should never follow his or her own opinions or preferences but always follow the principles of health, harmony and balance in handling public affairs, whether religious, political or financial. Lao Tzu mentioned several times that it is valuable to govern your life to make it be a peaceful and orderly world. He teaches the principles of how to handle our own lives. Within a person, there are many different elements which become harmonized for smooth function and happiness. We value the union of all the parts of the bodily life.

We can apply the same principle of internal government to our relationships with the world. This principle can be applied internally and externally. We do not need to search for a new system or set any other standard for the world. The best politics is the same as your healthy psychological experience of everyday life.

The world has become artificial and unnatural. Politics, religion and economic policies are all artificial; none really benefits human life. Attaining the well-being of each individual is the way to attain the well-being of society. The well-being of society is the application of the same principles as the *Book of Changes and the Unchanging Truth* and the *Tao Teh Ching* that we follow for our own individual person. The teaching of the Way and guidance I received reflects the problem of the world.

If we always talk about how to solve the problems of modern politics and religion, we will never find the way out and return to nature, so I am not going to talk about it too much.

My life experience is just like yours. We are not very different. I never received any special treatment from anyone or any society. I continue to talk about spiritual independence instead of recommending which church you go to or which religion you support.

The word Tao also seems not totally appropriate for my teaching, because there are other teachings which use the word Tao. My purpose in teaching is to serve the people of today, not to preserve the culture or teaching of yesterday. My goal is not to find a new audience for an old culture. I would like to join modern culture, the culture of today and the future, and not remain with the culture of the past. This is why I do not really use that old term too much.

Frank finishes reading.

III

Q: Master Ni, you said that we should not be too involved in politics, but neither should we passively accept incorrect government. Without becoming involved in politics, how can we effect the type of government we have to live under?

Master Ni: I would like to start by answering the first question which was asked before the reading. You see, we can do government by ourselves, bank for ourselves, worship by ourselves. We can bring all social functions inside our own domain. Now how will we operate it? There are two levels. Spiritually, one level is that your own growth will make a complicated system or complicated life become much simpler. Simplicity is an achievement; it is not a free gift. The second level is what I have already suggested to all the people from Atlanta; help me write some guidebooks about different aspects of life, such as how to use money, how to earn money and use it correctly, etc. Guidelines can be developed for all the practical things my books did not touch, but only gave principles for. They will be guide books about different subjects, such as how to eat, how to have relationships and so forth. These are all big matters.

I give all of you the assignment to make good suggestions, and then gather them together. My advice is given somewhere in my books; added together with your opinions, it may put in the newsletter which everybody has a chance to review and work on until it is accepted as the unified guidance of all. This is the best application of the subtle law. Then you will have some guidance for various situations in your life.

We like to make life simple, because life today is not simple. A person needs a lot of people with different training to help one's individual life. Life is too complicated; this is why I promote self-government, and that we come together to achieve it.

Now I will answer the second question. We do not need to point out the errors or shortcomings of our government, but we need to find a new way to do things. Constructive advice can be given to handle all kinds of trouble; after it is used, then there will be no trouble at all. Trouble and conflict can be prevented from even happening by using a special way to handle it.

So we come together during this time to examine how we can govern the practical aspects our lives. Offer this to people who are close to you and eventually we will influence the government, and slowly we will influence the world. I do not say that we should not respect the Constitution; it is supportive. But in this 200 years, too many unnecessary burdens have been created for each individual. We try to find a better, more simple way. This is how we can make a joint effort to make our lives more enjoyable. Then we will not need to spend so much time withstanding the pressures of society. What I want is for most people to enjoy their personal lives.

We do not need a revolution. We need to improve ourselves by applying what we would like to be. I would like you to really have a good program to offer everyone. We have all suffered and been troubled or bothered. None of that is your creation, but you are troubled. American society has become so complicated, nobody really knows anything, nobody really enjoys their life any more, because we all must put so much energy into our external livelihood and use a lot of energy to handle negative situations that are really not important.

When I talk about a world or a new society which has no litigation, my lawyer friends may all become nervous. However, they can still live better, because they can apply their energy into a different direction.

We need the world to be governed by the subtle law. The subtle law has no words. We need to apply the subtle law to our lives. I will be the first one to join such a worldwide nation with no war, no litigation, living a life of no tension and no pressure. We know that we are doing a business; nobody can be put in a position forever, but we would like to have a nation under the subtle law. That is simple.

Q: If we address problems like environmental issues or AIDS or war, is there a priority or a most troubling problem in the world?

Master Ni: I would like to offer you some positive help instead of putting lots of time into discussing problems. Psychologically, if you talk about problems, you become more frustrated. If you simply direct your energy into a positive area and leave the negative background behind you, you will do more good. The worst things are religions and politics, but we do not want to just talk about that, because they are everyone's creation. We must do better, because we also inherit their spirits. If we work toward improvement, we can be happy.

Q: So we should focus on what we can offer, which is to show a good way to live?

Master Ni: People who suffer come to you, but we should not only show the dark corner. People already know about that before they come to you. They come to you for guidance out of their darkness.

IV

Q: Master Ni, I would like to know more about your focus on the importance of spiritual independence.

Master Ni: A person who has one religion will only receive the help that the religion provides. Each religion has a different nature. If all religions say, "Believe in us and you will be helped," then the more religions you believe in, the more help you will receive. Surely you can enjoy the variety, just like enjoying all the good dishes that are put on the table. If you enjoy more, that is your benefit.

However, if you wish for spiritual growth and transcendence, you need spiritual independence before you can enjoy the variety. If you only eat one type of dish in the morning, afternoon and evening, it means you do not have spiritual independence.

If you are looking for the deep truth of all religions, it is better to keep to yourself and cultivate your own spiritual center rather than becoming scattered in unimportant things. Your physical body, mind and spirit are the foundation of high development and evolution. Look directly for the development of your physical health, mental strength and spiritual life.

Q: Master Ni, spiritually, Western society was once monopolized by a single religion. Now, its time is gone and gone also is the time when people did not have to think deeply. Now, we suddenly face many different teachings. It is difficult for a beginner to know what is right. It is your service to help us know more. You guide us to the depth of spiritual learning. What is your attitude toward religion?

Master Ni: My view is that there are too many religions in the world, and no one religion can serve world peace. The most important thing in the world is peace for all people. The negative side of religion causes confusion and prejudice because if you have faith in them, it affects your character and you are no longer able to embrace the entire world as part of your own life.

If somebody was to organize a crusade to kill people of a different faith, would you join? On some practical level, if you have a strong connection with the concepts of one religion, how can you be impartial? In the end, you are bound to take sides.

This statement I am going to make may bother you, but what you have attained as an open, healthy person will fail you if you go to a religion. Now, since the world has opened up to all cultures, it is a time of even more confusion because of a greater variety of spiritual teaching. We must still look for unity. Theories, doctrines and teachings bewilder people because their main purpose is to get more business, gain converts or gather people. If you listen to them and agree with something, then you create an inclination. Once your mind has an inclination toward something, then your internal spiritual and rational order are upset, the special natural order is violated and you are no longer in balance. You do not have equality toward all religions.

On a certain level, all religions give some service for certain people. If you consider some religions better than others, your mind is no longer centered.

All types of strange practices take you far away from your original truthful nature. All people who actively participate in religions pick up a religious standpoint. I would rather keep to my own truth of life and stay alone with the natural truth. I am not afraid of other people gathering as a group to speak their own language. If, under Heaven, the truth exists, it is one truth. That is the

Integral Truth which practices no discrimination at the conceptual level.

You do not need to force or bend the natural truth which is contained within your own life to fit the external form of certain sages or prophets. You have your own spiritual nature, and your responsibility is to stay with the crystal clarity of your own spiritual nature without allowing anything to disturb it.

Buddhism says, if you follow Buddhism, you shall become Buddha. Other religions say, if you follow the spirits, you shall become a spirit. However, for me, if I become a Buddha or a spirit, it is solely my own business; it can never be some other person's business.

Buddha is a name. Achieved ones already know that you cannot become a Buddha unless you work on yourself. Zen Buddhism started with this as the core of its spiritual teaching. Buddha nature or self nature is your own spiritual nature, and God or spirits are also terms for pure spirit. To say that God is good or God is truth expresses a certain spiritual quality that you know. If you wish to experience that reality, you have to clean yourself inside and out and move toward good. Never be puzzled by terminologies, because names are false. For example, a beautiful woman can be called Mary, but she could also be called Julia. There is no true relationship between the person, personality, spirits and the name. The purpose of a name is social. Deeper spiritual things do not need the external form of a name because having a name can be so rigid.

The heavenly kingdom of Jesus and the nirvana of Sakyamuni were spiritual solutions for all people, but even the best description is external, and thus not as good as directly returning to your own spiritual center. Heavenly kingdom and nirvana are terms which describe the reality of your own refined and achieved spiritual center, after you have accomplished spiritual learning and decide to keep open to all without losing the spiritual centeredness of life. Instead of studying descriptions, go to your own spiritual center. Then you will realize that the heavenly kingdom and nirvana are actually within you; they are your spiritual center.

If you do right and gain what is right, you participate in the reality of sagehood or godhood.   Sagehood is not external, like a name or position, which are irrelevant. Popular prophets and messengers of the past gave you their spiritual expression in their prophecy and messages. These were their own spiritual expression at that time rather than that of God, who lies beyond the human world. The real God is still far beyond their service.   If you accept the prophets or their expression, it is the expression of the time and of someone.   It is still not God.

Ancient prophets continue to influence present society through new leaders who use their framework or teachings. In a sense, the sages engage in social service because they have spiritual attainment.

In religions there is a huge variety of theoretical development, narrative description and cultural creations, but no single thing connects with the ever lasting spiritual center.

This has the same importance for all people, for you and me and the sages, who are all the same.   We need to straighten our road, change our way from going down to going upward and brush away the side attractions.   In your own life, can you see your target or goal?

The Way was passed down by the truthfully achieved ones.   If you are looking for the same achievement as them, you need to restore your pure spiritual essence. You do not need to search far for it.   The achievement or attainment of the pure spiritual essence is under your own foot; you must simply discipline and refine your own spiritual energy. Once you discover that you have the power to achieve the several thousand mile trip, you still need to step out to benefit other people. The right source of power enables you to reach the destination of your great realization.   The whole journey is totally your own responsibility; do not allow anything to confuse you.   You must do it all by yourself. Talking is of no use.

Q: Master Ni, I am slowly beginning to understand you now. However, can you say it a little more clearly?

Master Ni: If you join a religion, then you may have a downfall, because you "need" something external. I am saying that external faith is not internal growth. You can overcome this "need"; your need is your internal insufficiency. The carrot is hanging on the stick to make the donkey run. Do you need to run after the carrot for lifetimes? Instead of following a carrot, you need to look for your own enlightenment. Enlightenment enables you to return to your true self, your spiritual center. Those who cannot see this are like the person standing in the water who says "I am thirsty, but there is nothing to drink." He could not see the good water around him.

When people gather together, it is easier for corruption to start. Crowd-type energy may pull you away from clarity. Most people do not like to be isolated, but they like to join the fun and shallow interests. However, having fun with a group of people will cause you to lose your own personal depth. Your meditation, cultivation and independence are important because these things are done when you are alone.

Religious followers like crowds. They cannot live alone because they have not achieved spiritual independence. However, if you follow all types of external attraction such as a religion, your spiritual life will never be built up.

People join spiritual learning or join a religion with the original purpose of benefitting their souls, but the result is the opposite; they fall spiritually. If you are still not clear on this point, please review this chapter again, so that you can actually start to grow your own spiritual fruit.

Q: It seems that now I understand the importance of spiritual independence. I have also become more appreciative of the teaching of the Way, which is not a religion. Am I correct?

Master Ni: In order to follow the Way, a person needs to straighten up his or her spiritual and physical life. Straightening up your life means to lessen one's dependence upon external things. This is important because if anything you depend on becomes lost, it is hard for you to return to the spiritual center which is insubstantial, but is there and is more important than substantial things. We want our insubstantial spiritual center to be clear, not occupied by forms such as images, numbers or calculations. Once you attain this type of insubstantial mentality, your true energy will return to you.

In the morning, if you have returned to a life of truth or returned to your insubstantial spiritual center, then in the evening if you are going to die, you die as a person of natural truth, someone who is not confused by anyone or anything else.

Spiritual learning is so straight, but people make it crooked. I can only really talk to those who understand the truth about spiritual cultivation and spiritual development. Such a person knows at least, "It is I who needs to learn, it is I who needs to be achieved, it is I who needs to improve." You reach the subtle truth through learning, achievement and improvement. After you have a calm, clear, unoccupied mind, you can reach spiritual truth.

When you were a baby, you ate whatever your mother fed you. Now that you are a young man or woman, can you trust the world to feed you what is good for you? It is valuable to look for spiritual independence so that you can choose the right spiritual food to support your personal well-being and the healthy growth of your spiritual self.

Spiritual independence is a goal which cannot be slighted due to the pursuit of worldly fashion. Spiritual independence expresses a level of spiritual maturity. Personal spiritual cultivation is the way to attain spiritual independence.

Spiritual independence does not disagree with any one religion or with all religion as a whole. Spiritual independence means that you take charge of your own spiritual development; it is something you do for yourself, because no other person can achieve for you. However, being independent spiritually does not mean that you do not need a teacher or good books to help you. Spiritual independence also does not mean that you cannot have friends or participate in activities with a group of friends who pursue the same goal. Spiritual cooperation and mutual spiritual help among people are a better choice than the spiritual dominance of old religions.

A spiritually developed person knows to respect what prophets, sages and messengers have done to help others, and knows that now it is his or her turn to offer similar help. After attaining a reachable level of spiritual maturity, he or she might choose to engage in spiritual leadership.

Q: How can I achieve spiritual independence?

Master Ni: In order to achieve spiritual independence, you need to maintain your purity and your cleanness. Do nothing that would harm your composure. Do not be greedy for external things. Internally, be serene. Externally, be straight in movement.

Inspect the contents of your mind. Cut off any unimportant side interests or inclinations, because these only cause scatteredness. Make that energy return to the center, then remain concentrated to nurture your power. Practice clear and empty mindedness, which means not to be occupied by anything. Follow these truths:

Your ear should not be attached to amusing speech.

Your eye should not look for religious stimulation or other attractions. The purpose of all types of temples or altars is to attract your energy. However, it is better for you to use your life energy to tend your own 'temple' and 'altar' with your own earnest, honest life nature rather than attend to the altar of another person. Surely, no one needs to be so extreme as to do away with all external altars or temples; their positive function is to remind us of our own positive spiritual direction.

Always keep your heart and your mind in the right place. Guide yourself away from the internal thieves and all extra desires. As you learn to live following these guidelines, you will come to live a Godly life.

Your spiritual energy is within your physical energy, and your physical energy is within your spiritual life. Thus the yin and yang integrate and everything is correct. The life energy of the body and mind produce two kinds of spiritual energy which are called spiritual mercury and spiritual lead. With these two kinds of energy, one's whole internal energy will flow smoothly. When all channels inside have been opened up, there is no more internal obstacle, and you enjoy a happy, healthy, prosperous internal world. This is how you start to achieve the reality of spiritual independence. The purpose of spiritual independence is to attain the essence which is the most reliable spiritual element of your achieved spiritual being.

Student A: Master Ni, I have been bothered by the behavior of religious leaders. I really doubt that evangelists are spiritual models for people or true spiritual leaders of society. The occupation of evangelists is to give spiritual direction to people. However, it seems that they ignore the religious or spiritual purpose of life to practice a kind of salesmanship. What do they do with all the money and power they gather?

Student B: In this democratic country, the first amendment to the constitution gives all individuals free personal expression. Is free expression right or good for people who lack self-discipline? Can there still be a peaceful and orderly world if people are not righteous and straight?

Student C: People do not feel safe in all big modern cities because they fear physical attack. How did the world come to be like that? It seems to me that it is the natural downfall of the quality of people and the quality of culture.

Master Ni: Thanks for inspiring me; I would like to conclude this discussion with some final thoughts about politics.

The logrolling system, which is politicians helping each other by reciprocal voting for each other's bills, has prevailed for 200 years. Democracy should create fewer mistakes than a monarchy, yet, a wise monarch can do more for a country's people with less effort. In the Chinese region, in ancient times or at least more than 2,000 years ago, a wise king or emperor always consulted with a group of advisors or elders who were the wisest among the people before deciding a policy, issuing an order or enforcing a command. This consultation might result in the use of spiritual tools such as the *I Ching*. Why did the leader take so much trouble to make a decision? Because he knew his position was so influential and the decision would affect people's lives. He respected his position as that of God and he dared not do anything wrong, so the emperor fulfilled his spiritual nature. People also fulfilled their spiritual natures, and thus a time of peace was a time of prosperity. People knew that if their king or emperor was wise, they would live happily.

Objectively and conservatively speaking, good politics still depends upon positions of power being filled by good people. Therefore, out of love for the world and people, I advise each leader who issues policy or who influences the executive branch of any government to have personal moral discipline and be serious to develop themselves spiritually. The internal spiritual quality of leaders needs to meet the healthy quality of a society. With spiritual development, differences between individuals and political parties will be fewer. Any disputes will be only about how they can do more and do better for their country, instead of how they can obtain more for their party or their own personal political benefit.

Independent judgement and evolution on any matter can be nurtured through the attainment of a developed spiritual vision. It takes moral courage for any leader to share his or her deep vision with all others, to have it be understood and to create the opportunity for this vision to be accepted and implemented. It is my wish that all of you as individuals and leaders do your best toward the success and acceptance of this effort of helping others. In doing so, you must remain objective and selfless; this is the best way to offer public service. It means you do the work, but the success belongs to all people.

Now we only have one or two minutes left. During these two hours we have had lots of discussion about politics. If I were to put all of you here into the government, one of you as the American president, and others as senators and representatives, I believe the government of the United States would become even better. However, if you were to stay in such a political position, and if you did not look at my books any more, I am not sure you would be able to keep your high spiritual quality, because there are so many special interest groups who would like to influence you. If you wish to be elected, you have to spend lots of money; not only your own, but also the donations of special groups. This donated money then would make you become somebody's puppet. Independence does not mean to be a puppet, but to keep your own back straight. If we live a true natural life, with true heart and natural spirits, and our life spirit carries over into our politics, then there is hope.

Now it is time for lunch. Thank you, all of you, for coming. Some new friends have connected with me; I hope we will enjoy spiritual unity forever. Everywhere, you can find me in you and I can find you in me because spiritual unity can be found in each other. Practically, we need to work; not for only ourselves, but also for the world. Most of you are good people. You do not make trouble for the world, but the world makes trouble for you. You suffer and the next generation will suffer too. This is why I recommend that we eat well, so then we can laugh well.

Chapter 6

Forest Speaks

A Better World Starts in the Community

We are not an old religion, but we do correct the mistakes and problems of old religions. We are a spiritual path which has been in the world for thousands of years. People have ignored the essence of spiritual life and attached themselves to untruthful religious structures. Now it is time to turn back to the spiritual truth which is ever existent. That is the Integral Way.

The mission of the Integral Way in modern times is to teach and guide each person to become a complete person. A complete person has the following qualities: a universal heart, a healthy body, a clear and pure spirit and an educated but unconditioned mind.

When you try to make social progress through political administration, it is hard to get people to agree to move to a new direction. The Integral Way is both old and new. With the spiritual awakening of some people on a small scale, we might live a life of spiritual advancement by spiritual cooperation. Practically, I mean social change and improvement.

I would like to discuss a number of things for our future direction. First of all, there is the initiative spirit of the ancient sages such as Fu Shi, Shen Nung and the Yellow Emperor. This is called the Integral Way. Sages can never pass their sageliness to someone and make that person equal to themselves. In a new time, new sages come to respond to the world. Yet we can still identify spiritually with the ancient sages who exhibited the same ageless truth of life as the newcomers. We can also identify spiritually with the forefathers of the United States who promoted a new goal of human life with such qualities as independence, freedom, equality and justice for all people.

I would like to see marriage between the ageless Integral Way and the principles of new sages such as the forefathers of America and their new vision of human society. You can consider it a marriage of an old tradition with a new culture. This is the integration of the heritage of the *I Ching, Tao Teh Ching,* the Declaration of Independence and the Constitution of the United States on the spiritual level. We need mutual help to make this understandable to people. It is not a marriage but a continuation, because immortal spirits never die, they come back to the world again. At least, spiritually, the same initiating spirits like those of Fu Shi, Shen Nung, the Yellow Emperor and Jesus can come back, spirits of eternal life, everlasting life. All sages come back.

The ideal is to have a human society with equality, independence, freedom and justice for all people. However, the application of this ideal in American society is not complete. Besides the original goals of the American forefathers, we need to add the goals of mutual help, security, no riots and no crime. These things can only be attained through the spiritual development of each individual. Without spiritual development, independence, freedom and equality are all useless. They only provide more slogans to support personal aggression instead of helping people. Therefore, we say value the new sages, the American forefathers, and their vision of a new world and a new life, but let us never can forget the natural spirits for better survival.

If you call the teaching of the Integral Way Taoism, I do not accept that. My teaching is an old teaching integrated with the vision of the American forefathers to become a spiritual path, not a political government. So far, the government has not totally followed the spirit of its founders. The new politics is moving in a direction that is different than that which was set by the forefathers, thus new troubles have arisen. We need change and we need reformation.

The second part of this talk pertains to leadership. Leadership is similar to old-fashioned hero worship. A hero would come to town and do something, but then when he goes away, the bad thing comes back again and evil forces become active again. If we rely on leadership of one strong individual or party, then downfall will eventually occur. That kind of old social system needs improvement.

My suggestion for my own community, the society of Integral Wayfarers, applies to its leaders and mentors. I would like them to know one system, which I suggest. Even if we have some managers or coordinators who put everything together, we prefer subtle, open leadership which does not dominate.

Mao Tse Tung is an example of dominating leadership. He held political and military power. He could kill anybody who disagreed with him. This happened under Stalin as well. Besides political ambition, both of these men also had a humanistic motivation. Without that, they would never have been accepted by people. However, because the evil in their hearts was not seen, their power brought untold tragedy to many other individuals of humanistic heart. We should not continue to play the game of hero worship or rely on that way of life.

Today, in China, many people worry about the death of Deng Shao Ping. With his death, people do not know what will happen in society; they expect that disorder will come. We can strive for everlasting leadership, which is the leadership of the subtle law. Everybody can serve the realization of the subtle law in life. Whether personally or in society, please follow the principle of openness and subtlety. Avoid domination. We call it open, because it accepts all good ideas. A good idea does not necessarily come from a leader, it can come from any member.

The next thing, is not to establish or promote oneself or one's image like Hitler or Napoleon did. That will bring the trouble; sometimes it will also bring the disbenefit of destructive problems to society. If a system is good, it does not rely on a single leader; the leader can die or be changed, but the virtue of the system remains.

Astrology also has its influence. If something is to be accomplished in the world, it depends upon a specific energy. Some people become good leaders, some people become rich, some people become noble and are well respected; this is because the personal natural energy is there. Once the person uses up all the energy, then their achievement is scattered. We have seen the richest people in the world, but their descendants are not necessarily rich, because they are not as creative. Also, at the beginning of each new dynasty, the forefathers are creative, building a new society, nation or new peaceful order for society, but later generations deteriorate.

I have seen a businessman selling crabs by the basket. The big crab is put on the top of the basket, and the small lousy crabs are on the bottom. We are expecting the new generation to be better than ours, but it is like the basket of crabs: as you take one crab and then another, each one is worse than the one before. We would like each generation to do better than the previous one.

Even though the American system is different, the leaders of the new generations seem to have less spiritual and moral motivation than their predecessors.

Q: During the last ten years there seems to have been a revolution in American business management. Instead of keeping all of the authority in the hands of the managers, presidents and vice presidents, they give power to the workers so they can make decisions on the spot to serve the customers better. This is a new trend that is sweeping across America in terms of business management. I think this is what you are saying about not concentrating power centrally but rather spreading it to every single person that is involved. That makes the companies more profitable. This comes from the orient.

Master Ni: This type of management actually reflects Lao Tzu's teaching. Lao Tzu says the nobles are on the top, but the foundation comes from the bottom, not from the top. Remember, we still need leadership, management and coordination. Any good ideas that come from the bottom can be accepted by leadership. They may be well observed, well selected, well judged, well recognized and then unified to present to all the people. What you talk about is right; if a sentry is sent out, he needs to be authorized to do whatever he needs to do, but still have the connection with his superiors.

Q: There is a system set up so that they can operate freely within that system.

Master Ni: I shall appreciate your working out the details about open leadership replacing the dominating and one-person-all-power type of leadership.

The second thing I would like to talk about is the relationship between my teaching and the government. If a society or government wishes to make a change, it is difficult, because there are too many people involved. After three, five or even ten years, you do not see any change. However, radical revolutions are also not appreciated. Change can easily be made by a small group like us. We can establish a new better life and better world, because we have our vision.

For example, the central control of the Chinese communist system makes it ineffective. As Maoshing just mentioned, the new government can let the bottom manage itself. I am talking about a new society. I have already pointed out that the American forefathers valued independence, freedom and justice for all people. They did not mention the importance of mutual help and security for all people. They did not say that nobody can start a riot or harm other people's houses. Perhaps they did not see the importance of a society of no crime. Such a thing could not be fulfilled by a big society such as a government, but such a thing can be fulfilled in our small community.

So I would like us to make a system for the security of all of you who work for me. I am concerned about your security. Although we have a moral motivation in the world, I would like to have a system like a new society. It gathers money for the benefit and real use of all people.

Yesterday we discussed self-government. A person of self-government might think, "I am the government of myself, I am the bank of myself. I am the military defense of myself, I am everything of myself." It can be similar in the new community. Everyone has the independence, yet cooperation is the authority among all independent individuals. Cooperation can hardly be fulfilled by a big society, but it is easily fulfilled by us. If possible, by stages, I would like you to organize a society of mutual help with security. If you have money, then you put money into it; if you have talent, then you put talent into it. When you are old, you are cared for. We can use the example of the Chinese family. In the Chinese family system, everybody works but nobody claims ownership. It is natural that when the father and mother are old, they are taken care of by the children. There is no need for social security or anything else. The parents selflessly and devotedly guide their children when the children are young. I think some people make it into a crazy religion, but it is really a spirit of life to help one's children develop, because life is a continuation. When you are old, your children can stand up for themselves. Thus you do not worry about being old; you only need to make the young birds strong. I hope that people who contribute to society will be cared for in their old age.

I would like you to reform the commune system which says, "We are all equal, so everybody needs to spend equal time working on the land." They do not see that some people have less physical strength and other people have different intelligence. They do not respect individual or spiritual individuality.

You can have a community of joined or associated wealth in which the people in community all become wealthy. Everybody enjoys material comfort and does not suffer from poverty. All receive good training and good education, but they discipline themselves. In this new community that you are going to build, people do not need to stay together. They can live in different places, because today, communication and connection can all be made by computer.

For example, not everyone can develop themselves as excellent investors, but you can find a good group of investors to do the investing for the security of the old age of the workers or members. This can first be applied to the mentors only; then, if it is good enough, we will think about how to develop this system to extend to the members.

In the future, we may suggest this system to the government - or you may never need a government to do it, because in such a new society, the whole world will be as one nation. The whole new world will have no war and the new society has no litigation. How can you achieve it? This is the job of your group.

I am talking about the relationship with the government. It is easier for us to fulfill our hope by ourselves than to wait for the government to do it for us. It also cannot be fulfilled by one individual, but can only be accomplished if we organize together.

We mentioned that through knowledge of fortune or astrology, you cannot expect everybody to be born with the affluence of a king or queen. You cannot expect everybody to have an equal fortune, but a good system will save people. For example, in ancient times, in a natural society, if people's fortune was bad, they became beggars; if their fortune was good, they become dukes or landowners. You can see that where the democratic social welfare has been applied in northern Europe, those countries have no beggars. Even in China there are no beggars, but they also kill the initiative of people. We need to adopt a new system.

The Integral Way is the everlasting spirit of life and of all people. In each generation, we can practically inspire people in that direction. We not only recognize the ancient achieved ones, we also need to recognize all the sages whose names we do not even know. They must have a humanistic spirit to look for a good life for all people.

Because the community is small and the communication system is so well developed, it enables us to cooperate with all other small communities and make the world as one nation. You can project your universal heart for this to come about.

Conventionally, religion, politics and your personal life make three angles. Politics protects you physically if you pay taxes. Religion provides a social connection and also serves your spirit, but you pay a price for it too. The third angle is individual life. When these three are divided, they become a burden because they do not function well. You need to carry all of them in your life whether they function correctly or not.

However, now I am talking about your own operation of religion and your own political need. These can all be under your individual responsibility. All individuals can join and cooperate together to find the new way.

We recognize the sages of different times and different countries as our spiritual inspiration and spiritual ancestors. You might ask me whether or not we would include Karl Marx. Karl Marx originally wished to promote communism for all people, but he ignored the fact that capitalism stimulates people's creativity. An equal distribution system kills the motivation of personal achievement and individuality. We like the balance point between diversity and unity. Whatever makes variety exist also makes unity exist among the variety. Variety does not need for each dish on the table to compete with the other ones. We can recognize different customs, different ways and different stages of growth; that is all okay. We enjoy unity, yet at the same time we appreciate variety so we can have different good dishes. Everyone has personal preferences, but at the spiritual level we need unity. Unity is the humanistic universal heart. Universal love is unity.

The universal one divinity is spiritual unity. Even if she has her religion and he has his, neither one can deny the universal divinity. That is the unity.

So we respect and allow variety; we like it. If there is no variety, the world would be boring. You can have variety of creation, but also respect the unity.

We respect individuality, not the communist way of deindividualizing each person. We respect the expression of your personal interest and your personal development, but we still respect cooperation. Human cooperation is for better survival. If a person is not born with the destiny of a king, a rich person or someone very exalted in the world, under the new system he will not need to worry. With the new system, he could enjoy himself almost as greatly as a king or a rich man. I am not talking about physically, but in terms of life security. How? By a system. We can work on this system.

It is hard for us to look for the right person who has excellent fortune to achieve everything for us. Yet, we can set up a right system in which each person can work and function differently.

Is this the problem of Jesus, who could come back to make world peace for us? We might expect somebody to come along and do it, but nobody comes along. You and I have come along, so we need to organize a better system, the best system which can support us during our times of undevelopment, low cycle or bad fortune when we otherwise would not do well. It takes all kinds of effort to eliminate negativity and make the world be free from natural misery and from artificial political misery or tragedy. We can help eliminate all the misery and tragedy in the world. Let us begin by eliminating human self-created artificial misery, political misery and some natural misery.

Chapter 7

Earth Speaks

Better Individuals and Better Society

Student A: I think that in general all of us have seen a lot of the negative side of religion. It is difficult to say whether the world would really be better off without religion. Religion has declined rapidly in the United States since I was a child, and what seems to have replaced it is competition and greed rather than higher consciousness, despite higher education and the best standard of living in the world! I never cared for society much to begin with, but now it is a living hell. Frankly, I liked it better when people were more religious - they were kinder and more polite, and there seemed to be less misery in terms of crime, drugs and disease.

I do not see the value of tearing down religion - it only seems to let peoples' animal nature loose. Once those people head in the animal direction, they cannot turn around, much less become interested in a spiritual path that is higher than religion. Thus, although the common man's experience of religion is limited, it still serves a spiritual purpose that is suited to the level of the people who follow it.

The majority of people are not self-governing. Thus, to me the question seems to be how to direct people in a positive way so that they leave you alone and don't kill you on the highway because there is more horsepower at their fingertips than there are brains in their skulls. I honestly think religion is the only thing that can restrain and uplift them, to a point. Only when they reach the tip of the buffalo's horn can you tell them to turn around and come out in the open to see the light. If they don't see the darkness for themselves - say after a few thousand lifetimes - they aren't going to listen to anybody who says they're headed in the wrong direction.

Student B: I respect your reflection. Now, we have more religions than ever, but does this mean the world has become better? No one should dream that simple religious control could make the world better. If that were the case, then Italy would have no crime. Someone said that the Vatican itself is a big crime syndicate; it is uncertain how things developed to be that bad.

Years ago, society was safer because the free spirit of the Protestants made more progress than the control of the Catholics. Singular religious control did not bring social order, but people understood being dutiful in their lives. Now the Protestants have lost their function as a good model of behavior.

The new direction for how to improve our spiritual life is to have better, correct spiritual education. Truthful spiritual education can make people recognize the importance of being dutiful in their lives and respecting other people's lives. Religions are unable to do it, because they are regional customs. They are an obstruction to universal harmony and unity.

Progress cannot be made by controlling people, but only by helping people develop, grow and have better vision to see the world and see themselves. All of us can contribute to the world we live in. That is what we are working toward. Once people treat or put their religions and customs in proper perspective, they will engage in spiritual cultivation and activity.

Student C: We would rather follow universal spiritual education than one narrow religion. Human society paid dearly for religion, but received little service. I would like to give the following examples.

Historically, the Catholic church cooperated with rulers to exploit people's life fruit and block the free expression of their souls. Catholicism became the darkest social system in the entire human society.

People who had different spiritual experiences and different expressions of the same spiritual reality were considered pagans by the Catholic church and burned. Who authorized them to persecute people? The untruthful establishment of Catholicism is based on two elements: scheming and lying. It has obstructed human spiritual development and intellectual development, and interfered with the natural growth of all people.

The aftermath of the Catholic church was deep. The scatteredness and unhealthy condition of society was a reaction to the unnatural rule and discipline of the Catholics. People no longer knew how to handle their decent lives. When people of general society suddenly became developed intellectually, they did not have the experience to handle two weapons: their own intellect and the killing weapons invented by their intellects. This resulted from the unnatural building of society by forcible religious activity which interfered in all aspects of life.

Another example of dependence on social control is seen in politics. Communists say that they are fighting the evil of capitalism, but in reality they are reacting with antipathy to the cooperation between churches and rulers. Lenin learned the scheme of ruling from Catholicism; he applied the same cruel ruling by using new dogmas and a new god.

Master Ni: Truth itself is omni-present; it can never be monopolized by any one religion or any government.

When individuals and society itself restore their original organic condition, human society will be rescued. Based on that, we can look into further direction of useful and healthy development. It is clear that the fundamental direction of spiritual education and self-cultivation is to attain spiritual development which can support people's self-government.

1. Self-Government

The self-government of all people, all communities and all societies is not a pipe dream; it is a direction. Some people cannot make the distinction between a dream and a direction. I believe those people are accustomed to living in a society shackled under an artificial system of inhumane ruling which has existed during the past two thousand years of history. That was not the crown of human culture, but a disgrace.

Only dreamers hold the imagination of living in another place which is Heaven, so they help develop religions with such a promotion. Dreamers believe that their lives will become safe only when all people are controlled, but they do not see that control cannot solve the problem because when people are ruled, their spirits remain undeveloped. People cannot stay forever under a system that keeps them at the stage of cattle under herdsmanship. All historical signals show us that the application of herdsmanship culture to human lives should be finished.

Self-government does not mean people do not need to have a government in their society. It is necessary to have a government to run public affairs. The elected leaders of a government lead a group of specialists to accomplish special assignments or mandates voted for by the people. The government must be founded upon the base of each individual's personal self-government. By this I mean that the base comes from the bottom up. The base is not from the top down. As Lao Tzu says, the bottom is the foundation of the highness. This is why each individual of each society must attain his or her own self-government.

Public government consists of a group of different trained specialists who function as coordinators and workers of towns, cities and counties to fulfill regional needs. They are hired by the municipality or county. They are supervised by the few elected political leaders who manage for the efficiency of the specialists. In other words, a specialist government is based on special knowledge and training of individuals who perform functions as required for the people. With a specialist government, there will be no more politicians who are so active, make so much noise and know nothing about truthful and objective governmental service and function. It means that voters hire specialists to do all kinds of jobs such as city manager, etc., to run the government instead of politicians who run for office as a social leader.

There is no need for such figures of strong, social-political dominating leadership in a healthy, organic society. With the existence of politicians and politics, rivalry begins to exist among people: there are parties and people with special interests who try to influence the government of specialists. The specialists are only required to fulfill their duties objectively based on the requirement of reality, and not according to anybody's preference. No one group should influence these specialists. They are responsible for the good and correct function of the administration of public affairs.

When the government consists of people of special knowledge and training, they are hired to take care of public affairs, and then there will be no rivalry for such a position; thus, there is no splitting of society's unity. All people will enjoy great harmony by rendering positive mutual help for one another in everyday life. In such a society, any people who have political ambition can go to school to become one type of specialist in governmental service. There is no need for political rivalry as exemplified by one Chinese leader who killed many other political leaders in a bitter political struggle. Some old human societies have not yet finished with their haunting ghosts of emperors or czars. This type of tyrannical leadership and the establishment of ideological governments must be finished and replaced by specialists who can do some good for society.

The new epoch can be a time during which such a government of experts is hired and contracted to do the job for the interests of the people. Nobel prize winners or winners of any better program than the Nobel prize will be chosen and given jobs in key governmental positions. During the new epoch, political positions will no longer be for personal vanity or swollen egos. No noisy amateurs will sit on the chair of vanity or false glory and risk the security, prosperity and future of society. The new epoch needs real heroes in the field of practical improvement of human life. The new epoch needs no more unhealthy individuals who organize in groups to hinder the natural progress of humankind. For a long time in human history, individuals and groups have planted seeds of trouble. All types of work for society and for the individual need to be accomplished by good people. Good people are self-governed. We need good people in all levels of society. Do you think that a bus driver of a public or a private company should be an exception? Nobody should be an exception; everybody can have self-government and self-discipline in all levels of human society. This also means that it is not necessary to rely solely upon external discipline and that external discipline does not function over individuals all the time.

Useful specialists are not built only in a classroom or library. They grow in the field, with "real world" experience, with the assistance of the schools. Students of social science, for example, can participate in social activity and special investigations in order to learn about certain aspects of problems such as the economic or political aspect, etc., and find the cure. Later, they can apply their knowledge to the real problems of society. Professors and teachers eventually stay with society and the marketplace or business world more than personal study in order not only to make a theoretical report, but eventually to find a solution without political influence. Such study and educational investigation can have the cooperation of all people in society for the better fortune of all.

The position of independence of educational research and study can be recognized and respected. The resulting discoveries would help improve work quality at all levels, for example, as well as help provide fair payment for the workers. Situations such as waiting for the recession to cause a strike to break up, or workers being burnt in a factory because the door of the factory was kept locked until work hours were over could be things of the past. Problems can be dissolved in an informal and invisible way when trouble is small.

Teenagers in this country under 16 are not allowed to work. Yet they could be encouraged to learn the family trade or to learn housework. Do not push them out unprepared in their teens or twenties. A good artist usually develops skill during the teenage years. For all those with special achievements, at least some type of interest was built up and developed during the teenage years. This is the golden age to learn, because then people have a strong memory. This is especially important because many tend to destroy that strong memory with alcohol or social drugs. If teenagers learn anything good, they will remember it for their whole lifetime.

Drawing upon my own personal experience as an example, I started to learn my family trade at the age of 10. I developed the gentle martial arts interest at a similar age and at the same time, I developed the Chinese prediction system. Almost all my interests at that time were the foundation for my later development. If people do not learn to use their minds and hands when they are teenagers, they become clumsy after their twenties and have to work harder to achieve less compared to the imitation capability of the teenagers. In my hometown, most teenagers already joined their father's trade or did side work on the farms. There were no gangsters or delinquents in my hometown. Young people have lots of energy, but if they are not guided correctly in learning, I think they are misshapen, undeveloped like a beautiful garden left untended.

I would like to say that in the market, store, farm or office, young faces can join the family in work, not for serious life support but for their life training. It is not only a good custom, it is really useful for the young generation.

However, self-government is not only an external effort. Self-government is an internal effort of developing oneself and truly understanding one's duty toward other lives. Without individual spiritual development, there is no foundation for self-government and humanity can only live under external rule, which is a shame and disgrace.

My promotion of self-government of individuals and societies is based on the *Esoteric Tao Teh Ching* as universal spiritual advice for everybody and every society. Without serious learning and following the *Esoteric Tao Teh Ching*, the self-government of the world is false and irresponsible.

People who cannot govern themselves are not qualified to be "independent people," like the drunken drivers on the highway, unless they refuse to stay in the same stage as cattle by self-improvement and spiritual development. As long as people still expect some external authority to make a better world for them, they will still remain like cattle on a big ranch and argue about whose faith is better.

2. True Spiritual Life

People who are serious in spiritual development or in arranging their spiritual life would feel that politics is external attraction. It does not serve a spiritual purpose unless its activity is related to benefit many people. Politics can be practical; it should not be idealistic or ideological. Spiritual learning can be truthful in order to support real life in the world. Political leaders do not need special achievement, but they need to be practical and learn from the practical world through the experience of worldly affairs. There are so many people who compete for leadership. Modern politics is almost like a situation in which too many cooks spoil the broth.

It is necessary for most people to concentrate upon their spiritual life. If everybody would do that, the world would be peaceful and politics would become a minor thing in life.

Lao Tzu's teaching talks about the internal kingdom. People, no matter how high their social stature or position, usually leave their own life kingdom untended. It is the self-negligence of their own lives; meanwhile, they imagine that they are fixing the world. In reality, the way to fix yourself and the way to fix the world is the same path. Neither one should be neglected.

The physical life of each individual is easy to recognize as a life. A small or big society is also a life itself, the same as an individual. In both cases, there should not be much interference with the organic condition of the living entity. Similarly, the mind of an individual life as well as the leaders of society's government must learn to restrain interference with the body or society. The truth which supports this can be proven through spiritual attainment.

Chuang Tzu says, "First govern your own life; when you govern your life well, all three levels of your life are in good order. Then, when you have spare energy, you can help the world." Unfortunately, too many people neglect their own internal kingdom but forcibly push themselves to receive external recognition and gain. This wrong direction of human culture has existed for a long time. If more people were spiritually developed, then Lao Tzu's and Chuang Tzu's direction - spiritual contentment and enjoyment in one's own natural being - would be valued and exalted.

3. Apply the Principles of Government to Your Own Life

I am not particularly interested in politics or government. When I talk about them, mostly I mean the government of your internal kingdom. However, people who engage in spiritual self-cultivation are not isolated islands; they can have spiritual activities which also bring benefit to the health of society. This is the direction in which I am pointing.

Spiritually developed people know it is monkey business to sit on a throne and over-expand their egos, because that does not bring gain to life. That is spiritual sickness. When spiritual people make a political contribution through a position of public service, they like to offer their own life energy for the benefit of other people. They do not like to compete. They like to be accepted, but they are not annoyed if no one listens to them.

Therefore, the transcendent attitudes of spiritual people are applied to their own worldly life, but they also transcend that and offer whatever type of service is useful or appropriate to others. Spiritual people transcend the world because their attitudes are higher than the circumstances of life such as family life, business life, social life and various social involvements. However, if you are not involved, how can you talk about transcendence? From real life in the world, you nurture the transcendent spirit; in other words, you do not become attached to personal gain. You succeed in your spiritual wholesomeness, which is the gain above all.

4. Healthy Society

People of self-government offer their knowledge unselfishly through education and communication. They promote the great understanding of most people with the high spiritual principles we have discussed here. They help the world move in a great harmonious direction. They consider citizenship in universal self-government as their social obligation and offering toward realizing a healthy organic world. However, their main focus never moves away from self-improvement and decent self-discipline. They exercise spiritual qualities within themselves and attract the same spiritual qualities in other people to construct the new orderly natural organic world so that all people can enjoy the great heavenly kingdom on earth, not by one religion but by all religions and all customs. No one custom or religion will deviate from the Great One Path of Natural Truth. No one would lack the knowledge of the universal subtle law in their personal and business life.

A good society consists of people working to restore their natural virtue as angels or gods. It is not necessary to consider a god or angel as a special being or as a decoration of human spiritual culture. This is to say, "gods" or "angels" are not necessarily only spiritual beings or a decoration of human spiritual culture.

5. All Religions Can be Receptive to the Universal Subtle Truth

Generations of people over-relied on the false education of religion to make them good. However, once general people progress in their intelligence, the religious control is broken up. This breakup creates or causes a syndrome or becomes the aftermath of previous religious control.

Two thousand years have been wasted because of untruthful external establishment. Religions made no big real benefit, but only caused wars or created excuses for non-achievement because of weak-mindedness. In the past, religions could only offer the shadow of the roasted chicken on the dinner table. They did not bring a harmonious world to people. People paid too much for too little.

Religion was implemented irresponsibly in the first place. It was not a truthful teaching or foundation for building human society. We have witnessed that within these last two hundred years, when people became more intelligent, they broke away from false religious teachings. If a place has social discipline because of a strong police force, it is not a safe place to live. There is no safety because individuals do not discipline themselves. It is a shame when people only do right because they are surrounded by watchdogs. To rely on social discipline is superficial and shallow. No one should believe that society can provide all the answers, solutions, or protection; or that society has a separate, omnipotent presence. If there are no healthy individuals, there will be no healthy society. In truth, unnatural building of religion (religious education and their disciplines) did not truly help people, because it was superficial control.

The intellectual development of spiritually immature people is like small children playing with sharp, heavy knives and axes; inevitably they will hurt themselves or others in the end. My warning is that people need to thoroughly learn the natural spiritual truth which can be understood through my work in order to realize the direction of a harmonious world. We must do away with all obstacles, be they historical, social or individual, to find the true being of human life and restore natural health. Natural development can then be added to natural life. If we do not do away with obstacles to add natural development, we merely continue the behavior of religious dreamers who set up a ruling system and make themselves the special privileged class. This happened in conventional and communist societies. Whether a ruling system happens because of religion, royal court or one-party rule, the same darkness is expressed because it creates a specially privileged class. None of them is any better than the others.

The old type of religious establishment promotes strong ruler worship. One god symbolizes the high ruler. The church usurped the belief and became the rulers. This promotion was the deep and hidden spiritual disease of human society. A healthy world order is not the same as an external establishment like a religion which has one god and many gods above all other people. The religionists can wake up to one universal subtle law under which all beings and things are equal. A good world is one in which all people share equal responsibility in managing themselves and their contact with others.

The deepest sin of religious culture was not teaching truth to people and not assisting the growth of people. Instead religions applied schemes, lying and persecution to control and mange other people. That is not culture or the best reality of human life.

No one can expect the old type of religious control to come back to modern society. People must learn the truth of natural life from the Way and retrace the original, pure, simple nature of life.

6. The Goal of a Better Life and Better World

This is a new epoch with a new mission and new accomplishment. With a clear vision, you can move in steady steps. Through spiritual learning and teaching, and developing comfortable and reasonable social systems, we will achieve the new orderly world of self-government of each individual and each society with a complete natural organic condition. The world will become a world in which all people serve and all people enjoy, and nobody will suffer for erroneous creations of past leaders.

I hope nobody considers this as a dream or merely an idea. Spiritually developed people, I mean the people who have broad spiritual perspective, already have no prejudice or hostility that would affect their natural harmony with other people. Developed spiritual people can organize themselves as a self-governing community and make an example for the rest of the people. They can live as a community, together or in different places.

An ancient proverb says, "When the gentle breeze blows in the air, it does not damage anything; all lives, trees and grasses bow to it." I wish such a new healthy culture could produce ample influence for the world's people who desperately need such useful high culture.

Religion is not the solution. Political parties with radical policies are not the solution. Individualism is not the solution, nor is totalitarianism the solution. Only the natural good life which is open with all good conditions supporting all healthy groups of people is the solution. Yet they need protection from self-corruption. Thus, spiritual cultivation is the essential part of worldly life. In a natural good life, all people offer dutiful support to their society. This can start with anyone who has listened to me or who reads this who wishes to exercise their talent and natural gifts. Otherwise, we shall still waste another opportunity to do a fundamentally good thing for the world.

7. Universal Citizenship

We have talked about self-government. This means citizenship of universal self-government which never engages in any indecent business or that which harms society's health.

Citizens of universal self-government cast their independent vote for the right person and policy of humanistic consideration toward the entire society. They do not cooperate with criminal governmental behavior of aggression or suppressing the minority, etc.; they support peace. They support punishment for those who disturb the peace and harmony. They are patriotic. They are loyal to people of humanistic consideration. They do not follow fashionable thoughts which have not been tested to be useful or helpful in people's lives. They do not establish preference for one leader or another, nor do they participate in one political party or another. Their political position is to support the healthy side of society and the world. They do not use riots, protests or other less useful methods to try to improve their government or society.

It is their knowledge that anyone who is put in a governmental position will not necessarily do better than their predecessors. Historically, when many political leaders were young, they thought they could do better than the leaders then in power. Then, after years of struggle, they became the leaders, but they proved to be not really better than the other leaders. This is especially true of political leaders such as Mao Tse Tung, Hitler, Stalin, etc. They killed all other political leaders, but they finally proved that they were not any better than the others. This is not a single event in history; there are many similar proofs of the shortcomings of human emotion which denies people and overvalues oneself.

We talk about self-government according to the deep vision of pioneer teachers like Lao Tzu and Chuang Tzu. We do not like to unvirtuously expand ourselves over others. If this happens, the shortcoming of one's personality becomes the disaster of society. Human society has suffered long from leaders' bad personalities. From this truthful knowledge, the value of self-government can be clearly seen and recognized as trustworthy.

Citizens of universal self-government do not require people to be the same as them. They give up the thought of using force to make people appreciate their way or turn to their way. They live a life according to the natural model or model which is harmonious with all. They do what is right, by themselves and as their own society or group. They never extend their force to make people think or act the same way. They do not yield responsibility but constantly promote the great understanding of a healthy worldly life. Never discouraged, they extend their persistent work and their lives to help all people attain a greater understanding. Once this great understanding has reached people, the previous worldly struggle can be replaced by peaceful cooperation. They live in the Way, befriending all people, but they feel safest when other people share their understanding. Life is not a struggle for them, but life is internal and external work to reach the stage of balance, health and peace of all elements that support individual self-development and the development of society.

A big country with a strong military force offers to fulfill the role of international policeman in the time of need. As I see it, that can only be applied occasionally. Also, the big burdensome military budget could be used to bring about other important contributions. It cannot be considered as the solution for world peace and orderliness. The big budget could be used to educate all people to be aware that the only possible solution is the self-government of each society and community, which is based upon each individual's self-government.

Ancient developed sages such as Lao Tzu or Chuang Tzu did not know the word "democracy." Instead, they used the word "self-government" which offers the fundamental direction of human political and social relationships. It rejects the aggressive approach of any government or nations.

I appreciate a society of people's self-government with choice between independent life and living with a society more than the one choice decided by what is called "the majority," just like the communist society uses the word "people."

Let all people learn a good model of society, whoever establishes it. Politicians have their ideas. Any social leader can create a specific good model of society by gathering their family and friends together to produce the most orderly society. Each individual can enjoy his or her effective life under such a good system. Then, all people could learn from it. One does not need to impose ideas on others with fat promises or sweetened words.

8. The Integral Way

History has shown us that the world cannot be put in right order only through the establishment of religions or governments. Nor can the world benefit from individuals who set up ascetic disciplines for themselves. In order to work out a better world, we need both internal and external effort to meet one another.

The natural spiritual truth I promote is transreligious, which means that it is not only one religion or something that can be monopolized. We need the teaching of the Great Path of One Omni-Present Truth as the universal spiritual education which exists above all paltry religions and spiritual paths. Because the teaching of the ancient way is transreligious, it does not have an emotional relationship to any race or tribe; thus it is universal truth. It does not serve only one time, but it serves the spiritual direction of the entire world. Accurately speaking, people who are religious are not necessarily developed spiritually, but people who are transreligious have the opportunity to advance directly to the omni-present truth.

The Great Spiritual Path of Natural Spiritual Truth is the main spiritual guidance and direction for all people. People still can enjoy old customs or old religions as an incidental personal preference without letting them become an obstruction to spiritual unity with all people. Therefore, the spiritual education of the omni-present truth is not a religion of one God or many gods. It is a spiritual school of teaching all gods.

Self-government is the spiritual achievement of the individuals of society who are willing to practice self-discipline. There is still the need of a disciplinary system in society which is meant to help prevent transgressions of people who violate their own self-government and harm others. The self-government I recommend contains the essence of all different spiritual traditions. It is the achievement, inspiration and enlightenment accumulated during many generations of human ancestors.

The concept of 'spiritual self-government' from the unrealized old Chinese culture which I am promoting to the new world is the union of Universal Divinity with personal individuality. It is the realization of oneness of the Universal Being and your personal individual being. In other words, it is when the Universal Being and the individual being become one. It is the highest attainment of Indian religious devotion, and is called the 'Union of God and Oneself,' which is also unrealized by society. In Christianity, it is called 'Becoming One with Jesus.' In esoteric Buddhism, it is called 'Becoming Buddha Right in This Life.' In Chan (Zen) Buddhism it is called 'Instantly Becoming Buddha.' When applied in the individual sense, it is not enough.

True realization can bring about Jesus' Heavenly Kingdom, the Spiritual Paradise of Amitabha Buddhism, the future world with peaceful rule by Maitreya, the Buddhist Messiah, Confucius' world of Great Humanistic Love, etc. This types of paradise can and must exist right here in human society. However, not all religious paradises mean a better society. Some other type of paradises may simply hint at the death of life, only with decorative terms.

Now, new spiritual teachers and leaders can awaken to the simple reality of honest life and continue the footsteps of true sages and true heroes in the past, and not continue the footsteps of the liars of history.

Chapter 8

Mountain Speaks: Conclusion

In ancient times, the response of some sensitive people to the search for peace was to live in seclusion in remote mountains or rural villages. This attitude still exists in most spiritual traditions among those who are serious in their spiritual pursuit because world disturbance is unworthy and endless.

Seriously, however, what is the purpose of achievement? Is it just self-preservation or is it to exercise whatever you have attained from your spiritual cultivation to serve the public by improving the life of the majority of people? Practically, God is not selfish.

In conventional spiritual custom, godhood is similar to hero worship. A hero or a god is someone who can help others overcome a specific problem. Although this has never been achieved by anyone who is spiritually exalted, it is still a projection of human hope. We hope there is someone powerful enough to deliver the world from adversity and I do not think there is anything wrong with that view.

Sometimes spiritual people can be stubborn, like an ant entering the big end of a buffalo horn. As the ant enters the horn, it experiences more and more darkness and a darker, smaller and smaller tunnel until it cannot go any further. This is how modern or ancient people waste their lives by deciding to follow a spiritual path that leads them to seclusion in the mountains or a monastery, especially if they insist upon formalized ritual and a conceptual level of understanding. They never know that they are trapped inside a horn. Unless they have had any truthful warning from anyone else, they will think their choice is right. They think that no place is safer to live in than the horn. Yet, the horn has no exit.

In other words, some spiritual individuals avoid the world altogether. This is akin to a person entering the large end of a mine tunnel hoping to find gold. Continuing on, he experiences increasing darkness and a smaller and smaller tunnel until he cannot go any further. Finally, he is trapped and whatever gold might be found is useless. Following formalized ritual and a conceptual level of understanding are a similar trap, in which people never know they are trapped. They think it is a safe place, but there is no exit, especially in modern times.

On the other hand, there are spiritually interested individuals who struggle to live in society. They usually experience the same thing: society is also a horn with a dead end or a tunnel with no exit. Yet there are a few lucky ones - social leaders - who establish a system over other people so they themselves can enjoy the special privilege of being outside the system.

I would like to use a few practical examples to remind you of the possible downfall of the individual life harmed by leadership. During World War II, Japan suffered self-exhaustion from its over-expanded invasion. Because of this, Japan made its people suffer terrible material shortage and a poor life. They suffered poverty because of their leadership. Should those people be considered responsible for their poor lives? No, because the leadership caused trouble for the people.

Then, something worse happened. Two atomic bombs were dropped on Japan. One place in Chinese is called Guangtao (Hiroshima), and the other place is called Chang Chi (Nagasaki). Fortune tellers told the people who lived in those places during that time which of them would live long, enjoy a great future, or needed to suffer difficulty before reaching prosperity. No one told them that they would need to give up their lives for the atomic bomb, including the fortune tellers themselves.

The Japanese were devotees of Buddhism, but Buddha could not protect them. No divinity could deliver them from the national tragedy invited by aggressive leadership. That was 40 years ago.

Recently in Iraq, people lost their lives because of bad decisions of their leaders; no real benefit or military advantage was accomplished. South Africa has had a long unfinished struggle between the races. As a spiritual individual, I can only tell you that good leadership in society can bless your life. Poor leadership can make all people suffer. Leadership is always supported by a group of people and by itself does not singly do good or bad. Everything is done by people's choice. Spiritual cultivation is recommended for everyone, because it helps people maintain a calm objective view and distance from momentary events. However, if spiritual cultivation is over-individualized, or if it overemphasizes individual values or directions, it has no purpose.

While the leadership of society can cause you either to enjoy or suffer in life, the second most influential external element that determines the quality of your life is the political system of society. A good system can bring about a good life, and a bad system can make you suffer.

Therefore, I am emphasizing three things: individual improvement, good leadership and a good political and governmental system.

I am not talking about anyone sitting in a room or working in a library to design a system for all of us. There are still different preferences which do not depend on what is right, wrong, good or bad but depend on what people like, such as people who like a socialistic way of politics or non-socialistic way of natural life. I am talking about the importance of free choice. Some people prefer to live in a commune under a socialistic system or communism. Other people prefer individual responsibility to achieve what is needed in individual life and the maximum achievement of the individual that can be attained without violating the healthy social restraint. A natural society would not apply any restraint upon people of different but decent choice. In that way, people can get what they want. That is a real open society. Nobody else, even a leader or a government, should choose or decide for people, although the social protection of government is important to all.

This kind of open society has not been achieved by any nation. I am talking about a world society in which democracy, communism, monarchy, socialism and above all natural life, are not organized by force, but by people's own choice or preference. They are all operable at the same time if there is no harm caused by any one or another. Naturally, some systems cannot survive without using force. Those which need to use force to exist are bad and could be naturally extinguished. The premise of a social system is that it must be established by not using force or violence.

Talented people can organize as a company to offer whatever administrative job they can do for society. They can organize as different companies to replace political parties. The company can ask how much they would like to receive, what quality of job they can offer; thus, through the "bidding system" people can choose the less expensive and most effective one. The company cannot survive without fulfilling its promise or contract.

When your house needs to be reroofed or recarpeted, you ask different companies for estimates. Then you decide which company you will give the job to. You pay for the satisfaction of the material and the work.

Each company is organized by a group of managers and workers. Their budget is not made public but is considered their internal expense. The community hires them to fulfill the function of the administration. They are not specially privileged people, but they are just hired by the community. You can hire a foreign managing group too for better offers and better jobs. You can also organize your own group.

My personal related recommendation is that a society does not need a government as a ruling force, but as a group of managers. A society does need a group of managers who take care of specific work. The managers do not have any special or privileged position. They are responsible for what they do and they can adopt apprentices for their work to learn the details. The position does not change often unless the manager is unable to fulfill the duty.

If social leaders work for a specific department as managers, they would fulfill their duty and maintain their duty as an ordinary job not a special privilege. The boss is the people themselves. Everybody has an equal right to determine the quality of service of the managing group. It is not necessary to change the manager system but only to change incompetent managers. Managers have a right to report the pressure of special interest groups. Otherwise, they would be responsible for any wrongdoing and can be exiled from society for disloyalty. This is easier to fulfill in a small community; the example of a small community may offer a contribution for a better system in a large society.

The new tendency of democracy is to talk about the majority; then the majority suppresses or bends the opinion or choice of the minority. Yet, the majority of a democratic society does not necessarily carry the true opinion of the majority, because some people and the news media are active and influence the opinion of the majority. In other words, the opinion of the majority is not necessarily their opinion or choice. An open, natural society can respect individual choice as the highest right. A society can offer a political philosophical foundation such as independence, liberty, equality and justice for all people, but there might not be any trouble caused such as the majority suffering for the minority or vice versa. Each person would be allowed to make one's own choices to join different types of community life. All people can have their own discipline and growth, make their own choices and be allowed to change back and forth from different community systems.

In that way, people can live with different systems and still enjoy harmony. The government is authorized to protect the openness, freedom and safety of the society. Security and lifestyle are decided by each community's participants. Whether the majority or the minority creates trouble, the troublemaker can be severely punished. Because you already allow people to have free choice for different kind of life, you allow people to change their understanding from their own growth, so no one group of people can be aggressive and attack others who live differently. No group of people who do nothing can live on the fruit of other people's hard work.

Around 2,600 years ago, the wise Lao Tzu's focus was community life or a small kingdom which would live freely and happily with self-sufficiency. The community would find its own contentment, as would each individual in the community. I believe Lao Tzu's foresight of a smaller organic community of natural life is still a good vision and solution, without the clumsy burdens of a big society. States are not organized to cause trouble for themselves or any other state. I am still talking about Lao Tzu's kingdom. In smaller states, there are small communities. Each community disciplines its members to dissolve conflicts between individuals and with other states or communities.

A society can be organized for a better life with mutual help. All small communities can learn co-existence under a one-world government.

Spiritual people need not turn away from the world in order to build a better world. Your spiritual quality and service can all be fulfilled at the same time. Practically, spiritual achievement is fulfilled internally and externally at the same time. People who are talented and are naturally born leaders can use their life energy to create real benefit for human society, which includes their own lives, the life of their family and their descendants. They can selflessly follow the principles which I have offered the world.

I have dedicated myself to the new world direction for many years, but not only from my personal experience. I accept historical lessons, not as an individual, but as a person of universal mind. Since spiritual cultivation and development is my personal interest, whatever I have done in teaching is offered to all the beloved people of the harmonious universal one nation which enjoys high civilization and lives with a natural organic worldly order.

We need to value the individual. An interesting world is made of variety and difference. We must learn to respect variety and differences on the level of physical life. Even differences expressed by religions can also be accepted, but deep unity of the Immanent Way will always be valued.

I hope this is not just a dream of modern utopia, but can actually be fulfilled. I hope the world will be harmonious, not necessarily as I described, but even better. Surely there is always a better way when people make progress.

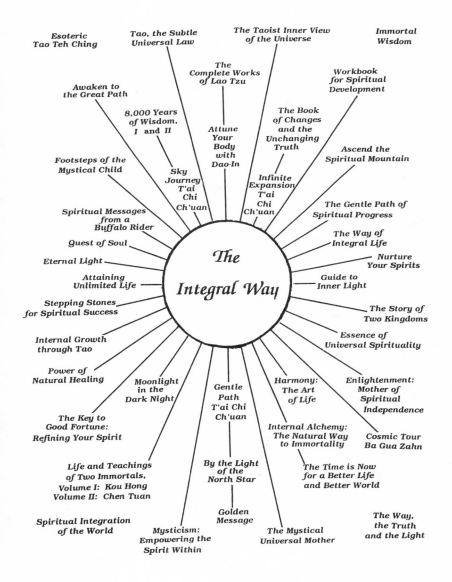

Esoteric
Tao Teh Ching

Tao, the Subtle
Universal Law

The Taoist Inner View
of the Universe

Immortal
Wisdom

The
Complete Works
of Lao Tzu

Workbook
for Spiritual
Development

Awaken to
the Great Path

8,000 Years
of Wisdom,
I and II

Attune
Your
Body
with
Dao-In

The Book
of Changes
and the
Unchanging
Truth

Ascend the
Spiritual Mountain

Footsteps of the
Mystical Child

Sky
Journey
T'ai
Chi
Ch'uan

Infinite
Expansion
T'ai
Chi
Ch'uan

The Gentle Path of
Spiritual Progress

Spiritual Messages
from a
Buffalo Rider

The Way of
Integral Life

Quest of Soul

The

Integral Way

Nurture
Your Spirits

Eternal Light

Guide to
Inner Light

Attaining
Unlimited Life

The Story of
Two Kingdoms

Stepping Stones
for Spiritual Success

Essence of
Universal Spirituality

Internal Growth
through Tao

Power of
Natural Healing

Moonlight
in the
Dark Night

Gentle
Path
T'ai Chi
Ch'uan

Harmony:
The Art
of Life

Enlightenment:
Mother of
Spiritual
Independence

The Key to
Good Fortune:
Refining Your Spirit

Internal Alchemy:
The Natural Way
to Immortality

Cosmic Tour
Ba Gua Zahn

Life and Teachings
of Two Immortals,
Volume I: Kou Hong
Volume II: Chen Tuan

By the Light
of the
North Star

The Time is Now
for a Better Life
and Better World

Spiritual Integration
of the World

Golden
Message

The Way,
the Truth
and the Light

Mysticism:
Empowering the
Spirit Within

The Mystical
Universal Mother

This list is according to date of publication, and offers a way to study Master Ni's work in order of his spiritual revelation.

1979: *The Complete Works of Lao Tzu*
       The Taoist Inner View of the Universe
       Tao, the Subtle Universal Law
1983: *The Book of Changes and the Unchanging Truth*
       8,000 Years of Wisdom, I
       8,000 Years of Wisdom, II
1984: *Workbook for Spiritual Development*
1985: *The Uncharted Voyage Toward the Subtle Light* (reprinted as
                  Awaken to the Great Path and
                  Ascend the Spiritual Mountain)
1986: *Footsteps of the Mystical Child*
1987: *The Gentle Path of Spiritual Progress*
       Spiritual Messages from a Buffalo Rider (originally
                  part of *Gentle Path of Spiritual Progress*)
1989: *The Way of Integral Life*
       Enlightenment: Mother of Spiritual Independence
       Attaining Unlimited Life
       The Story of Two Kingdoms
1990: *Stepping Stones for Spiritual Success*
       Guide to Inner Light
       Essence of Universal Spirituality
1991: *Internal Growth through Tao*
       Nurture Your Spirits
       Quest of Soul
       Power of Natural Healing
       Eternal Light
       The Key to Good Fortune: Refining Your Spirit
1992: *Attune Your Body with Dao-In*
       Harmony: The Art of Life
       Moonlight in the Dark Night
       Life and Teachings of Two Immortals, Volume I: Kou Hong
       The Mystical Universal Mother
       Ageless Counsel for Modern Times
       Mysticism: Empowering the Spirit Within
       The Time is Now for a Better Life and Better World
1993: *Internal Alchemy: The Natural Way to Immortality*
       Golden Message (by Daoshing and Maoshing Ni, based on
                  the works of Master Ni, Hua-Ching)
       Esoteric Tao Teh Ching
       The Way, the Truth and the Light
       From Diversity to Unity: Spiritual Integration of the World
       Life and Teachings of Two Immortals, Volume II: Chen Tuan

In addition, the forthcoming books will be compiled from his lecturing and teaching service:

Gentle Path T'ai Chi Ch'uan
Sky Journey T'ai Chi Ch'uan
Infinite Expansion T'ai Chi Ch'uan
Cosmic Tour Ba Gua Zahn
Immortal Wisdom
By the Light of the North Star: Cultivating Your Spiritual Life
Universal Spiritual Beings

About Master Ni

The author, Master Ni, says he is lucky; everywhere he goes, he gives lectures without speaking very good English and yet people listen and understand. Perhaps 10% of the communication is by understanding his words; the rest is his personal sincerity and energy. However, he feels that it is his responsibility to ensure that people receive his message clearly and correctly, thus, he puts the lectures and classes in book form.

It is his great happiness to see the genuine progress of all people, all societies and nations as one big harmonized worldly community. This is the goal that makes him stand up to talk and write as one way of fulfilling his personal duty.

What he offers people comes from his own growth and attainment. He began his personal spiritual pursuit when he was ten years old. Although his spiritual nature is innate, expressing it suitably and usefully requires world experience and learning.

When he is asked to give personal information, he says that there is personally nothing useful or worthy of mention. He feels that, as an individual, he is just one of all people living on the same plane of life and therefore he is not special. A hard life and hard work has made him deeper and stronger, or perhaps wiser. This is the case with all people who do not yield to the negative influences of life and the world.

He likes to be considered a friend rather than be formally titled because he enjoys the natural spiritual response between himself and others who come together to extend the ageless natural spiritual truth to all.

He has been a great traveller. He has been in many places, and he never tires of going to new places. His books have been printed in different languages as a side offering to his professional work as a natural healer - a fully trained Traditional Chinese Medical doctor. He understands that his world mission is to awaken many people, and his friends and helpers conjointly fulfill the world spiritual mission of this time.

BOOKS IN ENGLISH BY MASTER NI

The Time is Now for a Better Life and a Better World - *New Publication*
What is the purpose of achievement? Is it just self-preservation or is it to exercise whatever you have attained from your spiritual cultivation to serve the public by improving the life of the majority of people? Master Ni offers his profound vision of our modern day spiritual dilemma to help us awaken to combine our personal necessity with the better survival of universal society. 136 pages, Softcover, Stock No. BTIME, $10.95

The Way, the Truth and the Light - *New Publication!*
Of all teachings by famous worldly sages, the teaching of this highly exalted sage in this book expresses the Way closest to that of Lao Tzu. The genuine life of this young sage links the spiritual achievement of east and west which highlights the subtle truth. 232 pages, Softcover, Stock No. BLIGH, $14.95

Life and Teaching of Two Immortals, Volume 2: Chen Tuan - *New Publication!*
The second emperor of the Sung Dynasty entitled Master Chen Tuan "Master of Subtle Reality." Master Ni describes his life and cultivation and gives in-depth commentaries which provide teaching and insight into the achievement of this highly respected Master. 192 pages, Softcover, Stock No. BLIF2, $12.95

Esoteric Tao Teh Ching - *New Publication!*
Tao Teh Ching has great profundity in philosophy and spiritual meaning, and can be understood in many ways and on many levels. In this new previously unreleased edition, Master Ni gives instruction for spiritual practices, which includes in-depth information and important techniques for spiritual benefit. 192 pages, Softcover, Stock No. BESOT, $12.95

Golden Message - A Guide to Spiritual Life with Self-Study Program for Learning the Integral Way - *New Publication!*
This volume begins with a traditional treatise by Master Ni's sons about the general nature of spiritual learning and its application for human life and behavior. It is followed by a message from Master Ni and an outline of the Spiritual Self-Study Program and Correspondence Course of the College of Tao. 160 pages, Softcover, Stock No. BGOLD, $11.95

Internal Alchemy: The Natural Way to Immortality - *New Publication!*
Ancient spiritually achieved ones used alchemical terminology metaphorically for human internal energy transformation. Internal alchemy intends for an individual to transform one's emotion and lower energy to be higher energy and to find the unity of life in order to reach the divine immortality. 288 pages, Softcover, Stock No. BALCH, $15.95

Mysticism: Empowering the Spirit Within - *New Publication!*
For more than 8,000 years, mystical knowledge has been passed down by sages. Master Ni introduces spiritual knowledge of the developed ones which does not use the senses or machines like scientific knowledge, yet can know both the entirety of the universe and the spirits. 200 pages, Softcover, Stock No. BMYST2, $13.95

Life and Teaching of Two Immortals, Volume 1: Kou Hong - *New Publication!*
Master Kou Hong was an achieved Master, a healer in Traditional Chinese Medicine and a specialist in the art of refining medicines who was born in 363 A.D. He laid the foundation of later cultural development in China. 176 pages, Softcover, Stock No. BLIF1, $12.95.

Ageless Counsel for Modern Life - *New Publication!*
These sixty-four writings, originally illustrative commentaries on the *I Ching*, are meaningful and useful spiritual guidance on various topics to enrich your life. Master Ni's delightful poetry and some teachings of esoteric Taoism can be found here as well. 256 pages, Softcover, Stock No. BAGEL, $15.95.

The Mystical Universal Mother
An understanding of both masculine and feminine energies are crucial to understanding oneself, in particular for people moving to higher spiritual evolution. Master Ni focuses upon the feminine through the examples of some ancient and modern women. 240 pages, Softcover, Stock No. BMYST, $14.95

Moonlight in the Dark Night
To attain inner clarity and freedom of the soul, you have to control your emotions. This book contains wisdom on balancing the emotions, including balancing love relationships, so that spiritual achievement becomes possible. 168 pages, Softcover, Stock No. BMOON, $12.95

Harmony - The Art of Life
Harmony occurs when two different things find the point at which they can link together. Master Ni shares valuable spiritual understanding and insight about the ability to bring harmony within one's own self, one's relationships and the world. 208 pages, Softcover, Stock No. BHARM, $14.95

Attune Your Body with Dao-In
The ancients discovered that Dao-In exercises solved problems of stagnant energy, increased their health and lengthened their years. The exercises are also used as practical support for cultivation and higher achievements of spiritual immortality. 144 pages, Softcover with photographs, Stock No. BDAOI, $14.95 Also on VHS, Stock No. VDAOI, $39.95

The Key to Good Fortune: Refining Your Spirit
Straighten Your Way *(Tai Shan Kan Yin Pien)* and The Silent Way of Blessing *(Yin Chia Wen)* are the main guidance for a mature, healthy life. Spiritual improvement can be an integral part of realizing a Heavenly life on earth. 144 pages, Softcover, Stock No. BKEYT, $12.95

Eternal Light
Master Ni presents the life and teachings of his father, Grandmaster Ni, Yo San, who was a spiritually achieved person, healer and teacher, and a source of inspiration to Master Ni. Some deeper teachings and understandings on living a spiritual life and higher achievement are given. 208 pages, Softcover, Stock No. BETER, $14.95

Quest of Soul
Master Ni addresses many concepts about the soul such as saving the soul, improving the soul's quality, the free soul, what happens at death and the universal soul. He guides and

inspires the reader into deeper self-knowledge and to move forward to increase personal happiness and spiritual depth. 152 pages, Softcover, Stock No. BQUES, $11.95

Nurture Your Spirits
Master Ni breaks some spiritual prohibitions and presents the spiritual truth he has studied and proven. This truth may help you develop and nurture your own spirits which are the truthful internal foundation of your life being. 176 pages, Softcover, Stock No. BNURT, $12.95

Internal Growth through Tao
Master Ni teaches the more subtle, much deeper sphere of the reality of life that is above the shallow sphere of external achievement. He also clears the confusion caused by some spiritual teachings and guides you in the direction of developing spiritually by growing internally. 208 pages, Softcover, Stock No. BINTE, $13.95

Power of Natural Healing
Master Ni discusses the natural capability of self-healing, information and practices which can assist any treatment method and presents methods of cultivation which promote a healthy life, longevity and spiritual achievement. 230 pages, Softcover, Stock No. BHEAL, $14.95

Essence of Universal Spirituality
In this volume, as an open-minded learner and achieved teacher of universal spirituality, Master Ni examines and discusses all levels and topics of religious and spiritual teaching to help you understand the ultimate truth and enjoy the achievement of all religions without becoming confused by them. 304 pages, Softcover, Stock No. BESSE, $19.95

Guide to Inner Light
Drawing inspiration from the experience of the ancient achieved ones, modern people looking for the true source and meaning of life can find great teachings to direct and benefit them. The invaluable ancient development can teach us to reach the attainable spiritual truth and point the way to the Inner Light. 192 pages, Softcover, Stock No. BGUID, $12.95

Stepping Stones for Spiritual Success
In this volume, Master Ni has taken the best of the traditional teachings and put them into contemporary language to make them more relevant to our time, culture and lives. 160 pages, Softcover, Stock No. BSTEP, $12.95.

The Complete Works of Lao Tzu
The *Tao Teh Ching* is one of the most widely translated and cherished works of literature. Its timeless wisdom provides a bridge to the subtle spiritual truth and aids harmonious and peaceful living. Also included is the *Hua Hu Ching*, a later work of Lao Tzu which was lost to the general public for a thousand years. 212 pages, Softcover, Stock No. BCOMP, $12.95

The Book of Changes and the Unchanging Truth
The legendary classic *I Ching* is recognized as the first written book of wisdom. Leaders and sages throughout history have consulted it as a trusted advisor which reveals the appropriate action in any circumstance. Includes over 200 pages of background material on natural energy cycles, instruction and commentaries. 669 pages, Stock No. BBOOK, Hardcover, $35.00

The Story of Two Kingdoms
This volume is the metaphoric tale of the conflict between the Kingdoms of Light and Darkness. Through this unique story, Master Ni transmits esoteric teachings of Taoism which have been carefully guarded secrets for over 5,000 years. This book is for those who are serious in achieving high spiritual goals. 122 pages, Stock No. BSTOR, Hardcover, $14.50

The Way of Integral Life
This book includes practical and applicable suggestions for daily life, philosophical thought, esoteric insight and guidelines for those aspiring to serve the world. The ancient sages' achievement can assist the growth of your own wisdom and balanced, reasonable life. 320 pages, Softcover, Stock No. BWAYS, $14.00. Hardcover, Stock No. BWAYH, $20.00.

Enlightenment: Mother of Spiritual Independence
The inspiring story and teachings of Master Hui Neng, the father of Zen Buddhism and Sixth Patriarch of the Buddhist tradition, highlight this volume. Hui Neng was a person of ordinary birth, intellectually unsophisticated, who achieved himself to become a spiritual leader. 264 pages, Softcover, Stock No. BENLS, $12.50   Hardcover, Stock No. BENLH, $22.00.

Attaining Unlimited Life
Chuang Tzu was perhaps the greatest philosopher and master of Tao. He touches the organic nature of human life more deeply and directly than do other great teachers. This volume also includes questions by students and answers by Master Ni. 467 pages, Softcover, Stock No. BATTS $18.00; Hardcover, Stock No. BATTH, $25.00.

The Gentle Path of Spiritual Progress
This book offers a glimpse into the dialogues between a Master and his students. In a relaxed, open manner, Master Ni, Hua-Ching explains to his students the fundamental practices that are the keys to experiencing enlightenment in everyday life. 290 pages, Softcover, Stock No. BGENT, $12.95.

Spiritual Messages from a Buffalo Rider, A Man of Tao
Our buffalo nature rides on us, whereas an achieved person rides the buffalo. Master Ni gives much helpful knowledge to those who are interested in improving their lives and deepening their cultivation so they too can develop beyond their mundane beings. 242 pages, Softcover, Stock No. BSPIR, $12.95.

8,000 Years of Wisdom, Volume I and II
This two-volume set contains a wealth of practical, down-to-earth advice given by Master Ni over a five-year period. Drawing on his training in Traditional Chinese Medicine, Herbology and Acupuncture, Master Ni gives candid answers to questions on many topics. Volume I includes dietary guidance; 236 pages; Stock No. BWIS1   Volume II includes sex and pregnancy guidance; 241 pages; Stock No. BWIS2. Softcover, each volume $12.50

Awaken to the Great Path
Originally the first half of the *Uncharted Voyage Toward the Subtle Light*, this volume offers a clear and direct vision of the spiritual truth of life. It explains many of the subtle truths which are obvious to some but unapparent to others. The Great Path is not the unique teaching, but it can show the way to the integral spiritual truth in every useful level of life. 248 pages, Softcover, Stock No. BAWAK, $14.95

Ascend the Spiritual Mountain
Originally the second half of the *Uncharted Voyage Toward the Subtle Light*, this book offers further spiritual understanding with many invaluable practices which may help you integrate your spiritual self with your daily life. In deep truth, at different times and places, people still have only one teacher: the universal spiritual self itself. 216 pages, Softcover, Stock No. BASCE, $14.95

Footsteps of the Mystical Child
This book poses and answers such questions as: What is a soul? What is wisdom? What is spiritual evolution? to enable readers to open themselves to new realms of understanding and personal growth. Includes true examples about people's internal and external struggles on the path of self-development and spiritual evolution. 166 pages, Softcover, Stock No. BFOOT, $9.50

The Heavenly Way
A translation of the classic Tai Shan Kan Yin Pien (Straighten Your Way) and Yin Chia Wen (The Silent Way of Blessing). The treatises in this booklet are the main guidance for a mature and healthy life. This truth can teach the perpetual Heavenly Way by which one reconnects oneself with the divine nature. 41 pages, Softcover, Stock No. BHEAV, $2.50

Workbook for Spiritual Development
This material summarizes thousands of years of traditional teachings and little-known practices for spiritual development. There are sections on ancient invocations, natural celibacy and postures for energy channeling. Master Ni explains basic attitudes and knowledge that supports spiritual practice. 240 pages, Softcover, Stock No. BWORK, $14.95

Poster of Master Lu
Color poster of Master Lu, Tung Ping (shown on cover of workbook), for use with the workbook or in one's shrine. 16" x 22"; Stock No. PMLTP. $10.95

The Taoist Inner View of the Universe
Master Ni has given all the opportunity to know the vast achievement of the ancient unspoiled mind and its transpiercing vision. This book offers a glimpse of the inner world and immortal realm known to achieved ones and makes it understandable for students aspiring to a more complete life. 218 pages, Softcover, Stock No. BTAOI, $14.95

Tao, the Subtle Universal Law
Most people are unaware that their thoughts and behavior evoke responses from the invisible net of universal energy. To lead a good stable life is to be aware of the universal subtle law in every moment of our lives. This book presents practical methods that have been successfully used for centuries to accomplish this. 165 pages, Softcover, Stock No. TAOS, $7.50

MATERIALS ON NATURAL HEALTH, ARTS AND SCIENCES

BOOKS

101 Vegetarian Delights - *New Publication!* by Lily Chuang and Cathy McNease
A vegetarian diet is a gentle way of life with both physical and spiritual benefits. The Oriental tradition provides helpful methods to assure that a vegetarian diet is well-balanced and nourishing. This book provides a variety of clear and precise recipes ranging from everyday nutrition to exotic and delicious feasts. 176 pages, Softcover, Stock No. B101V, $12.95

The Tao of Nutrition by Maoshing Ni, Ph.D., with Cathy McNease, B.S., M.H. - This book offers both a healing and a disease prevention system through eating habits. This volume contains 3 major sections: theories of Chinese nutrition and philosophy; descriptions of 100 common foods with energetic properties and therapeutic actions; and nutritional remedies for common ailments. 214 pages, Softcover, Stock No. BNUTR, $14.50

Chinese Vegetarian Delights by Lily Chuang
An extraordinary collection of recipes based on principles of traditional Chinese nutrition. For those who require restricted diets or who choose an optimal diet, this cookbook is a rare treasure. Meat, sugar, diary products and fried foods are excluded. 104 pages, Softcover, Stock No. BCHIV, $7.50

Chinese Herbology Made Easy - by Maoshing Ni, Ph.D.
This text provides an overview of Oriental medical theory, in-depth descriptions of each herb category, over 300 black and white photographs, extensive tables of individual herbs for easy reference and an index of pharmaceutical and Pin-Yin names. This book gives a clear, efficient focus to Chinese herbology. 202 pages, Softcover, Stock No. BCHIH, 14.50

Crane Style Chi Gong Book - By Daoshing Ni, Ph.D.
Chi Gong is a set of meditative exercises developed thousands of years ago in China and now practiced for healing purposes. It combines breathing techniques, body movements and mental imagery to guide the smooth flow of energy throughout the body. It may be used with or without the videotape. 55 pages. Stock No. BCRAN. Spiral-bound, $10.95

VIDEO TAPES

Attune Your Body with Dao-In (VHS) - by Master Ni. Dao-In is a series of movements traditionally used for conducting physical energy. The ancients discovered that Dao-In exercise solves problems of stagnant energy, increases health and lengthens one's years, providing support for cultivation and higher achievements of spiritual immortality. Stock No. VDAOI, VHS $39.95

T'ai Chi Ch'uan: An Appreciation (VHS) - by Master Ni.
Master Ni, Hua-Ching presents three styles of T'ai Chi handed down to him through generations of highly developed masters. "Gentle Path," "Sky Journey" and "Infinite Expansion" are presented uninterrupted in this unique videotape, set to music for observation and appreciation. Stock No. VAPPR. VHS 30 minutes $24.95

Crane Style Chi Gong (VHS) - by Dr. Daoshing Ni, Ph.D.
Chi Gong is a set of meditative exercises practiced for healing chronic diseases, strengthening the body and spiritual enlightenment. Correct and persistent practice will increase one's energy, relieve tension, improve concentration, release emotional stress and restore general well-being. 2 hours, Stock No. VCRAN. $39.95

Eight Treasures (VHS) - By Maoshing Ni, Ph.D.
These exercises help open blocks in your energy flow and strengthen your vitality. It is a complete exercise combining physical stretching, toning and energy-conducting movements coordinated with breathing. Patterned from nature, its 32 movements are an excellent foundation for T'ai Chi Ch'uan or martial arts. 1 hour, 45 minutes. Stock No. VEIGH. $39.95

T'ai Chi Ch'uan I & II (VHS) - By Maoshing Ni, Ph.D.
This exercise integrates the flow of physical movement with that of internal energy in the Taoist style of "Harmony," similar to the long form of Yang-style T'ai Chi Ch'uan. Tai Chi has been practiced for thousands of years to help both physical longevity and spiritual cultivation. 1 hour each. Each video tape $39.95. Order both for $69.95. Stock Nos: Part I, VTAI1; Part II, VTAI2; Set of two, VTAI3.

AUDIO CASSETTES

Invocations for Health, Longevity and Healing a Broken Heart - By Maoshing Ni, Ph.D.
This audio cassette guides the listener through a series of ancient invocations to channel and conduct one's own healing energy and vital force. "Thinking is louder than thunder. The mystical power which creates all miracles is your sincere practice of this principle." 30 minutes, Stock No. AINVO, $9.95

Stress Release with Chi Gong - By Maoshing Ni, Ph.D.
This audio cassette guides you through simple, ancient breathing exercises that enable you to release day-to-day stress and tension that are such a common cause of illness today. 30 minutes. Stock No. ACHIS. $9.95

Pain Management with Chi Gong - By Maoshing Ni, Ph.D.
Using easy visualization and deep-breathing techniques developed over thousands of years, this audio cassette offers methods for overcoming pain by invigorating your energy flow and unblocking obstructions that cause pain. 30 minutes, Stock No. ACHIP. $9.95

Tao Teh Ching Cassette Tapes
This classic work of Lao Tzu has been recorded in this two-cassette set that is a companion to the book translated by Master Ni. Professionally recorded and read by Robert Rudelson. 120 minutes. Stock No. ATAOT. $12.95

Order Master Ni's book, *The Complete Works of Lao Tzu,* and *Tao Teh Ching* Cassette Tapes for only $23.00. Stock No. ABTAO.

How To Order

Name: _____

Address: _____

City: _____ State: _____ Zip: _____

Phone - Daytime: _____ Evening: _____

(We may telephone you if we have questions about your order.)

Qty.	Stock No.	Title/Description	Price Each	Total Price

Total amount for items ordered_____

Sales tax (CA residents only, 8-1/4%)_____

Shipping Charge (see below)_____

Total Amount Enclosed_____

Visa _____ Mastercard _____ Expiration Date _____

Card number:_____

Signature:_____

Shipping: Please give full street address or nearest crossroads. If shipping to more than one address, use separate shipping charges. Please allow 2 - 4 weeks for US delivery and 6 - 10 weeks for foreign surface mail.

By Mail: Complete this form with payment (US funds only, No Foreign Postal Money Orders, please) and mail to: Union of Tao and Man, 1314 Second St. #208, Santa Monica, CA 90401

Phone Orders: You may leave credit card orders anytime on our answering machine. Please speak clearly and remember to leave your full name and daytime phone number. Call (800) 578-9526 to order or (310) 576-1901 for information..

Shipping Charges:

Domestic Surface: First item $3.25, each additional, add $.50.
Canada Surface: First item $3.25, each additional, add $1.00.
Canada Air: First item $4.00, each additional, add $2.00
Foreign Surface: First Item $3.50, each additional, add $2.00.
Foreign Air: First item $12.00, each additional, add $7.00.

All foreign orders: Add 5% of your book total to shipping charges to cover insurance.

_____ Please send me your complete catalog.

Thank you for your order

Spiritual Study through the College of Tao

The College of Tao and the Union of Tao and Man were established formally in California in the 1970's. This tradition is a very old spiritual culture of mankind, holding long experience of human spiritual growth. Its central goal is to offer healthy spiritual education to all people of our society. This time-tested tradition values the spiritual development of each individual self and passes down its guidance and experience.

Master Ni carries his tradition from its country of origin to the west. He chooses to avoid making the mistake of old-style religions that have rigid establishments which resulted in fossilizing the delicacy of spiritual reality. He prefers to guide the teachings of his tradition as a school of no boundary rather than a religion with rigidity. Thus, the branches or centers of this Taoist school offer different programs of similar purpose. Each center extends its independent service, but all are unified in adopting Master Ni's work as the foundation of teaching to fulfill the mission of providing spiritual education to all people.

The centers offer their classes, teaching, guidance and practices on building the groundwork for cultivating a spiritually centered and well-balanced life. As a person obtains the correct knowledge with which to properly guide himself or herself, he or she can then become more skillful in handling the experiences of daily life. The assimilation of good guidance in one's practical life brings about different stages of spiritual development.

Any interested individual is welcome to join and learn to grow for yourself. Or you just might like to take a few classes in which you are interested. You might like to visit the center or take classes near where you live, or you may be interested in organizing a center or study group based on the model of existing centers. In that way, we all work together for the spiritual benefit of all people. We do not require any religious type of commitment.

The College of Tao also offers a Self-Study program based on Master Ni's books and videotapes. The course outline and details of how to participate are given in his book, *The Golden Message*. The Self-Study program gives people an opportunity to study the learning of Tao at their own speed, as a correspondence course, or for those who wish to study on their own or are too far from a center.

The learning is life. The development is yours. The connection of study may be helpful, useful and serviceable, directly to you.

- -

Mail to: Union of Tao and Man, 1314 Second Street #208, Santa Monica, CA 90401

_____ I wish to be put on the mailing list of the Union of Tao and Man to be notified of classes, educational activities and new publications.

Name:_____

Address:_____

City:_____State:_____Zip:_____

Herbs Used by Ancient Masters

The pursuit of everlasting youth or immortality throughout human history is an innate human desire. Long ago, Chinese esoteric Taoists went to the high mountains to contemplate nature, strengthen their bodies, empower their minds and develop their spirit. From their studies and cultivation, they gave China alchemy and chemistry, herbology and acupuncture, the I Ching, astrology, martial arts and T'ai Chi Ch'uan, Chi Gong and many other useful kinds of knowledge.

Most important, they handed down in secrecy methods for attaining longevity and spiritual immortality. There were different levels of approach; one was to use a collection of food herb formulas that were only available to highly achieved Taoist masters. They used these food herbs to increase energy and heighten vitality. This treasured collection of herbal formulas remained within the Ni family for centuries.

Now, through Traditions of Tao, the Ni family makes these foods available for you to use to assist the foundation of your own positive development. It is only with a strong foundation that expected results are produced from diligent cultivation.

As a further benefit, in concert with the Taoist principle of self-sufficiency, Traditions of Tao offers the food herbs along with the Union of Tao and Man's publications in a distribution opportunity for anyone serious about financial independence.

Send to: *Traditions of Tao*
1314 Second Street #208
Santa Monica, CA 90401

Please send me a Traditions of Tao brochure.

Name _____

Address_____

City_____State_____Zip_____

Phone (day)_____(night)_____

Yo San University of Traditional Chinese Medicine

"Not just a medical career, but a life-time commitment to raising one's spiritual standard."

Thank you for your support and interest in our publications and services. It is by your patronage that we continue to offer you the practical knowledge and wisdom from this venerable Taoist tradition.

Because of your sustained interest in Taoism, in January 1989 we formed Yo San University of Traditional Chinese Medicine, a non-profit educational institution under the direction of founder Master Ni, Hua-Ching. Yo San University is the continuation of 38 generations of Ni family practitioners who handed down knowledge and wisdom from father to son. Its purpose is to train and graduate practitioners of the highest caliber in Traditional Chinese Medicine, which includes acupuncture, herbology and spiritual development.

We view Traditional Chinese Medicine as the application of spiritual development. Its foundation is the spiritual capability to know life, to diagnose a person's problem and how to cure it. We teach students how to care for themselves and other, emphasizing the integration of traditional knowledge and modern science. Yo San University offers a complete Master's degree program approved by the California State Department of Education that provides an excellent education in Traditional Chinese Medicine and meets all requirements for state licensure.

We invite you to inquire into our university for a creative and rewarding career as a holistic physician. Classes are also open to persons interested only in self-enrichment. For more information, please fill out the form below and send it to:

Yo San University
of Traditional Chinese Medicine
1314 Second Street
Santa Monica, CA 90401

☐ Please send me information on the Masters degree program in Traditional Chinese Medicine.

☐ Please send me information on health workshops and seminars.

☐ Please send me information on continuing education for acupuncturists and health professionals.

Name _____

Address _____

City_____State_____Zip_____

Phone(day)_____(evening)_____

INDEX